KNOWING BRITTEN

Also published by the Bittern Press

Making Musicians:
A Personal History of the Britten-Pears School
Moira Bennett

Change of Key:
Africa to the Arts
Moira Bennett

Knowing Britten

Steuart Bedford

with

Christopher Gillett

BITTERN PRESS

First published 2021
The Bittern Press
14 Mill Lane
Campsea Ashe
Woodbridge
Suffolk IP13 OPL

Typeset by Agnesi Text, Hadleigh, Suffolk
Printed and bound in Great Britain by Indigo Ross, Sudbury, Suffolk

A catalogue record for this book is available from the British Library.

ISBN 978-0-9571672-2-3

FOR CELIA

The Bittern Press gratefully acknowledges the generosity of Christine and Simon Airey and an anonymous donor for their financial support of *Knowing Britten*.

Contents

List of Illustrations

Lesley Duff (Lucia) and Nancy Evans (Lucretia) in *The Rape of Lucretia*,
Glyndebourne, 1946.
Photo Angus McBean © Houghton Library, Harvard University; courtesy of Britten Pears Arts

Peter Pears (Albert), Lesley Duff (Emmie), David Spenser (Harry)
and Anne Sharp (Cis) in *Albert Herring*, Glyndebourne, 1947.
Photo Angus McBean © Houghton Library, Harvard University; courtesy of Britten Pears Arts

Steuart Bedford, *c.* 1970.

Between pages 146 and 147

Death in Venice, Snape Maltings, 1973: Robert Huguenin (Tadzio)
and Peter Pears (Aschenbach).
Photo Nigel Luckhurst © Britten Pears Arts

Peter Pears, Colin Graham and Steuart Bedford in the Piazza San Marco,
Venice, 1973.
Collection of Steuart Bedford

Janet Baker, Benjamin Britten and Steuart Bedford rehearse *Phaedra*, 1976.
Photo Nigel Luckhurst © Britten Pears Arts

Steuart Bedford conducting Janet Baker and the English Chamber
Orchestra in a rehearsal for the first performance of *Phaedra*, June 1976.
Photo Nigel Luckhurst © Britten Pears Arts; collection of Steuart Bedford

Rehearsal for *Canticle IV: 'Journey of the Magi'*, Festival of Flanders, 1974:
James Bowman, Peter Pears, John Shirley-Quirk and Steuart Bedford.
Photo Jan Nackaerts; courtesy of Britten Pears Arts

Janet Baker, Steuart Bedford and John Shirley-Quirk before a performance
of Wolf's *Italienisches Liederbuch* at the 1977 Aldeburgh Festival.
Photo Nigel Luckhurst © Britten Pears Arts

Steuart Bedford conducts a rehearsal of Brahms's Double Concerto
in A minor, Op. 103, with Isaac Stern, Mstislav Rostropovich
and the English Chamber Orchestra, 13 June 1982.
Photo Nigel Luckhurst © Britten Pears Arts

Steuart Bedford rehearses the English Chamber Orchestra, 1982.
Photo Nigel Luckhurst © Britten Pears Arts

Between pages 158 and 159

Murray Perahia, Steuart Bedford, John Shirley-Quirk, Heather Harper,
Sarah Walker and Marie McLaughlin rehearsing for a gala concert
marking Peter Pears's seventieth birthday on 22 June 1980.
Photo Nigel Luckhurst © Britten Pears Arts

Steuart Bedford with Marie McLaughlin (Tytania), backstage before
a performance of *A Midsummer Night's Dream* on 7 June 1980.
Photo Nigel Luckhurst © Britten Pears Arts

Benjamin Britten, Rita Thomson, Steuart Bedford and Lady Penn
at a reception after the 'Patron's Choice' concert on 13 June 1975.
Photo Nigel Luckhurst © Britten Pears Arts

Steuart and Lesley Bedford with Theodor (Ted) Uppman
after an orchestral concert at Snape Maltings, 19 June 1975.
Photo Nigel Luckhurst © Britten Pears Arts

Lennox Berkeley, Steuart Bedford (playing the harpsichord), Peter Pears
and Ian Partridge rehearsing on the stage of Snape Maltings for
a concert during the 1978 Aldeburgh Festival.
Photo Nigel Luckhurst © Britten Pears Arts

Steuart Bedford, Murray Perahia and John Ogdon during
the 1977 Aldeburgh Festival.
Photo Nigel Luckhurst © Britten Pears Arts

Steuart Bedford with Jonathan Miller at the 1979 Aldeburgh Festival.
Photo Nigel Luckhurst © Britten Pears Arts

Steuart Bedford with William and Susana Walton
at the 1979 Aldeburgh Festival.
Photo Nigel Luckhurst © Britten Pears Arts

Between pages 176 and 177

'*Grimes* on the Beach', 2013 Aldeburgh Festival: Steuart Bedford
in the pit during a rehearsal.
Photo © Christopher Gillett

Celia and Steuart Bedford, Florence, 1978.

Celia, Jo and Charmian Bedford, 1987.

Celia and Steuart Bedford, Crag Path, Aldeburgh, 2016.
Photo © Charmian Bedford

Steuart Bedford at home in Yoxford, 2018.
Photo © Christopher Gillett

Alun and Steuart Bedford, Aldeburgh, 2020.
Photo © Charmian Bedford

ONE

My mind beats on

Snape Maltings, 16 June 1973

It's noisy backstage. Not loud, but noisy. A multitude of sounds bounces off the white-painted brick walls of the narrow corridors. Singers are warming up in their tiny dressing rooms. Doors are constantly opening and shutting as well-wishers pass on their good-lucks. A Tannoy broadcasts the orchestra as it tunes, the xylophone repeating a tricky phrase over and over again.

The audience can be heard filing into the hall from the reeded banks of the River Alde; regular festival-goers, critics, the great and the good, all slightly reluctant to forgo the beauty of the warm, cloudless evening, excited to be the first to see Britten's latest opera, *Death in Venice*. It is, after all, a historic occasion.

It's no secret that Britten isn't well. Who knows if he will compose again? And the rumours about the piece . . . such a subject. Is this wise? Those hoping that Britten will defy expectations and appear in the box set discreetly in the brick wall of the auditorium for this world premiere will be disappointed. He is too weak, recuperating at Horham, his rural retreat on the Suffolk–Norfolk border, after his recent heart operation.

Peter Pears sits quietly in his dressing room, studying his score, pressing gently on Aschenbach's moustache, checking that the spirit gum will hold.

Over the Tannoy the stage manager calls for beginners. Out of the conductor's room steps a young man – just thirty-three – dressed in white tie and tails. Undeniably handsome, he has thick black hair and a general air of benevolence. He walks with a slightly swaying gait, and if stopped and asked a question, his head will rock back and his bright blue eyes widen and shoot upwards before turning in a slow roll to one side, as if searching the air for the answer.

He is shy but confident in what he knows, dismissive of half-baked opinions, wary of strangers, yet warm to his friends. Despite his slightly donnish appearance, away from the podium he will find the time and the technical know-how to rewire his house entirely by himself. He will conduct lengthy experiments to determine whether the milk should go in before or after the tea. He will consume vast amounts of chocolate biscuits yet never put on weight. He will never wear sandals without also wearing socks. He will state, privately, that the wonderful thing about the conducting profession is that 'if you stick at it long enough, people eventually think you're an expert'.

This is Steuart Bedford, tasked by Benjamin Britten to conduct everything and anything that, in times of better health, the composer would have certainly conducted himself. It's quite a responsibility, not to mention a burden of trust. But Steuart is unusual among Britten's professional colleagues – unique, even. Steuart might be only thirty-three but he has known Ben for nearly twenty-seven years. Steuart has known Britten since he was a seven-year-old boy.

Thorpeness, Suffolk, September 1952

IT IS A BEAUTIFUL, sunny afternoon in early autumn; perfect for an informal cricket match between Ben Britten's Eleven – his 'home side' – and a selection of locals and friends. As the players gather, all dressed in their whites, and wait for the toss of the penny that will decide who will bat first, groups of spectators, some carrying picnic baskets, wander to the boundary, seeking out the optimum location to watch the game. Britten wins the toss and opts to field.

Among the spectators is a striking woman, and with her, her three sons. She is Lesley Duff, a soprano. She has sung for the first three seasons of Britten's English Opera Group and become a familiar presence on occasions like this.

The three sons are: Peter, twenty-one, who is studying classics at Cambridge and who possesses a fine baritone voice; David, fifteen, a very keen cricketer who has won considerable laurels playing for his school, Lancing College, knocking up a century in his most recent match; the final member of the trio of boys is me, Steuart. I am thirteen. David has been invited to play in the match but my parents consider me too young for such an honour.

Piled up in the pavilion is a large haul of cricketing gear – pads, gloves, spare bats, balls, stumps and bails – all of it available to anyone who is playing. The more experienced hands who don't have their own equipment have shown up early to grab the best of the haul.

Padded up and ready to play, the opening batsmen are making their way onto the pitch along with the fielding side when someone rushes out of the pavilion and shouts, 'We don't have any umpires!' The first umpire, it seems, has been involved in a minor car accident.

As is common in amateur cricket, the number 11 player of the batting side is volunteered to be second umpire, but the match is still short of a first umpire. Consternation.

Just then, a middle-aged man, his mind apparently immersed in some deep problem, is spotted wandering towards the Bedford family group. Our prayers are answered. Despite his protestations that he knows nothing about the laws of cricket, the new arrival – my father, Leslie Bedford – is squeezed into a standard white coat, and pushed towards the first umpire's station at the non-striker's end, where he is quickly briefed by the second umpire on the more important rules of the game.

My father immediately gets off to a bad start when he fails to realise that he is supposed to check the batsman's guard before play can begin. Instruction is given, the guard is taken and the bowler, Peter Pears, sends down a fizzler, which the batsman ignores.

Thorpeness 1952. Peter Pears, Benjamin Britten, Henry Whitehead, Stewart Ogilvie, Lord Harewood, an unidentified man, and David Bedford, behind. Why Pears, a bowler, appears to be dressed for wicket-keeping is a mystery.

The next ball, however, crashes into the batsman's left pad, causing a loud shout of 'howzat'. A decision is needed from the inexperienced first umpire. If there's uncertainty, tradition dictates that the batsman gets the benefit of the doubt, but the cry from the field has been too strong for the umpire to resist, and after an agonising pause my father lifts his finger to shoulder height and the 'out' verdict is given. The batsman is obliged to leave the field and this he does, leaving a trail of fierce invective in his wake, all the way to the pavilion, where the stream of colourful language describing the stupid umpire and his ridiculous verdict becomes even stronger.

In the pavilion is my brother David, looking for a pair of batting gloves small enough to fit his adolescent hands. The disgruntled batsman, completely unaware that there is anyone else in the pavilion, lets forth another string of obscenities. As the feast of swearing continues, David manages to slip out of the pavilion unobserved and, rather shaken, seeks the security of his family. His mother senses something is amiss but is sensible enough not to probe. Whatever the problem is, it will no doubt surface eventually.

But the problem never surfaces. There really isn't a problem at all. No, David is far more interested in compiling a long list in his head of as many new swear words as he can remember – a list he will later share with me – courtesy of the 'storming batsman', or as he later discovers he is better known: Lord Harewood, a close friend of Britten, president of the Aldeburgh Festival, grandson of King George V and first cousin to the Queen.

I simply cannot remember who won the match. Perhaps Peter Pears demolished the opposition with his fast bowling, while Ben waited patiently in the slips for a catch. I cannot recall. When it was over, my parents said fond farewells to Ben and Peter and our family made for our holiday home in Snape.

◊

At the time of the cricket match Britten had known Steuart and his brothers for almost six years; since Boxing Day, 1946. He had known Lesley Duff, their mother, a few months longer, since their first meeting in May that year, when she auditioned for the role of Lucia in Britten's new opera, *The Rape of Lucretia*.

Born in 1904, Lesley Duff trained at the Royal Academy of Music. Her father was a successful painter, R. K. Duff, known for his watercolours, pastels and etchings.

My mother won all the prizes; she was the Academy's number-one singer. When she left, she was taken up by Eric Greene, a well-known tenor in those days, and she became quite friendly with him. The other person who helped her a lot was Steuart Wilson – note how his first name is spelled – who became deputy general administrator at

Covent Garden. He was also a tenor and, by all accounts, a very difficult man. She became quite well known on the oratorio circuit, also doing a bit of opera, the odd *St Matthew Passion*, that sort of thing.

In the 1920s, just a few years into her singing career, Lesley Duff met Leslie Bedford, an engineer and inventor, and in 1928 they married. Their son Peter was born in 1931, then David in 1937, and finally Steuart in 1939. Once she was married there was no pressure whatsoever on Lesley to provide income; she sang what she wanted to sing – Bach and Purcell for preference – and was never absent from home for long.

Only my great aunt disapproved of her singing after marriage, but my mother always tried to come home after concerts so she would be there in the morning. I have no recollection of her not being around.

Home was in Hampstead Garden Suburb in North London, though the infant Steuart was briefly evacuated to Devon during the Second World War. In the garden was an Anderson air-raid shelter and Steuart can still remember the sound of v-1 and v-2 flying bombs overhead. Meanwhile, Lesley Duff toured the country singing concerts for ENSA – the Entertainments National Service Association, commonly known as 'Every Night Something Awful' – where she struck up a good friendship with the pianist Viola Tunnard, who would later become one of Britten's key répétiteurs, thanks largely to an introduction from Lesley.

In 1946 the Bedfords moved to a large three-storey house close to Hampstead Heath, with a lodger and a live-in housekeeper. There the six-year-old Steuart started piano lessons, played cricket in the big garden with his 'bossy' older brother David, or helped his father Leslie build things out of Meccano in his workshop.

We made clocks and radios from kits. We sold one of the clocks to our local doctor. The first radio we built made no sound whatsoever when we switched it on. Then white smoke started to waft out of it and my father hastily switched it off again.

Leslie was the youngest son of Herbert Bedford, a composer and painter, and his mother was the hugely popular composer and singer Liza Lehmann, who counted Clara Schumann among her friends. Leslie's only brother died in training during the First World War.

Around the turn of the century, no self-respecting middle-class household lacked a copy of Liza Lehmann's *In a Persian Garden* on the parlour piano. The royalties from her 1917 song 'There Are Fairies at the Bottom of Our Garden' alone paid for Steuart's brother Peter's university fees at King's College, Cambridge.

During the war Leslie Bedford had worked on radar, inventing an elevation-finding device called the Bedford Attachment. He became chief television engineer at Marconi in 1947 and the company's historian described him as 'an almost legendary character, of immense intellectual stature, with a head like a minor prophet crossed with a Roman emperor, a disconcertingly direct manner and a fiendish sense of humour. Brilliant, unpredictable – sometimes outrageous – he can appear deceptively unworldly, but the feet of this "absent-minded professor" seldom leave the ground, however high in orbit his head may seem to be'.

My father could play the piano by ear. He could hardly read music. He could sit down and harmonise perfectly, correctly and musically, and he could play all the Gershwin numbers, which he loved. David got a saxophone once and they would play duets. He loved sailing but he wasn't a great sailor. Every time we went out we landed up on the mud. He would take his trousers off and jump straight over the side to push us into deeper water.

During 1948, while recovering from an operation on her neck, Steuart's mother, Lesley, wrote a private memoir, which she kept hidden in a drawer of her dressing table. It was found after her death in 1987 in a brown envelope labelled 'Just a diary, please destroy'. Whether she was serious in her request is open to question. Clearly, from the style of her writing, the memoir wasn't really for her eyes only. It reveals a singer struggling with her self-confidence, desperate for affirmation, probably on the cusp of early retirement, who suddenly finds herself, and her family, drawn deep into a heady new creative circle. That she fell in love with Britten is totally without question and, while not a direct confession, it was clearly a secret she wanted both to keep and to share. Her husband probably found the diary and read it. He certainly didn't destroy it. He probably knew his wife was infatuated but knew too that her infatuation would eventually come to nothing – an unspoken, badly kept secret. In post-war Britain, there were plenty of unspoken, badly kept secrets.

Reading his mother's memoir, forty years or so after she wrote it, is fascinating and troubling for Steuart. Troubling because her family – many of whom are unaware the memoir even exists – might get the wrong idea, or feel embarrassed by the strength of her feelings for a man who wasn't her husband. Troubling too that Lesley herself might be ashamed to have her infatuation shared with anyone but her notebook.

The audition in 1946 – for Lucia in *The Rape of Lucretia* – was so late, so close to the start of the production, that they must have lost somebody. Even though my mother was now forty, they clearly didn't know her. They must, I think, have turned to Eric Greene for advice and he must have suggested her. That's my guess. I don't think she had seen *Peter Grimes* at this stage, or knew that much about Britten. But later in life, the two things she said she wanted to do in life were to sing Purcell and Britten. The war would have put the brakes on her career too. And having three boys.

On Saturday, 4 May, Lesley Duff arrived early for her audition with the thirty-two-year-old Britten at his flat in St John's Wood. She wandered the high street and wasted some time shopping before finally ringing his doorbell and singing him some Purcell.

Ben evidently was rather ill-at-ease, rather abrupt, giving an impression of immensely strained youth. 'I hope you'll be with us,' he said. I said I had no idea what it was for. 'Hasn't anyone told you *anything*? It's a chamber opera called *The Rape of Lucretia*, written by myself, and we need two casts – you would be taking [i.e. doubling] Margaret Ritchie's part. I'll fetch it.'

And then in front of me was a proof copy of the Linen Trio – perhaps the most lovely, most ill-served piece of music he will ever write.

I didn't see him again till Whit Monday [10 June], our first day at Glyndebourne. He, with Joan [Cross] and his dear friend Peter [Pears], had only just arrived from Switzerland, and they all walked into the dining room late – looking wonderfully well and happy. I didn't realise then his desperate shyness and the terrible strain that that afternoon was to him.

'I am going to try and sing all the parts,' he said. 'If you simply can't bear it, please don't hesitate to go away. I shall absolutely understand, peculiar as my voice is.'

And that was how we first heard *Lucretia* – heart-breaking, wonderful *Lucretia*.

'Don't be afraid,' he would say continually. *Don't be afraid*, his eyes would say before a difficult passage. I never once, on any occasion, saw him out of patience with any one of us.

'I wish you wouldn't be frightened,' he said to me one day. 'Don't you know that I am so touched at anyone taking the trouble to sing my music, and am so grateful that I don't mind *what* you do.' Not strictly true, but in essence perhaps. At any rate, it's a very lovely thing for a young composer to make himself say.

Duff describes a cast member who, embarrassed that she is constantly getting a passage of the opera wrong, tries to avoid Britten.

'Don't you dare to run away from me! It's *my* fault for writing it that way – *all* my fault.'

He once said to me, 'If *one* thing goes wrong, I feel the whole opera's wrecked!'

After the run at Glyndebourne, *Lucretia* toured the UK and the Netherlands. In 1946 alone, it had a staggering 83 performances, many of which Britten conducted.

Conducting was then an immense strain to him. He was unsure of his conducting technique and got into a terrible state of nerves and sickness.

She was still an outsider, shy in his company:

I saw Ben only once or twice through the winter. Once on his birthday, sitting in the artists' room of the Central Hall [Westminster], his arms full of presents, like a very small boy. Then at Joan's Christmas Day party when he suddenly said, 'May I meet your boys? Can we come to tea tomorrow?'

Actually they came to lunch and it was Ben's first gesture to me of friendship and a desire to come closer and into my home. We were all a little shy I think, but the boys immediately sensed the true spirit of love and youth in Ben, and very soon there was ping-pong and a sense of relaxation, a very slow shedding of restraint. His charm with children is well known but with mine he seemed to walk into their hearts and be immediately accepted as beloved and special.

'He doesn't *do* anything about children,' Peter said to me. 'He just loves them, which is really all that matters.'

They took us to *The Fairy Queen* at Covent Garden that night. He got tense and strained, and now and again made wild sotto-voce outbursts. Not that they were so entirely sotto voce either. 'Never mind,' said Peter the comforter. 'Purcell will survive it.'

'Yes, but it's put him back at least fifteen years,' said Ben desperately. They took us out to dinner and were delightful, witty hosts.

He had invited the children to a party somewhat vaguely, and rang up the next day in great distress to say there had been a special meeting called of the directors of the English Opera Group. Would the children forgive him? He couldn't say how sorry he was – 'Please explain' – and he would come over himself the next day to bring them a record he had and make his peace. This was important to him. Making a promise to a child, and to have to disappoint or let down children, was a very real horror to him.

Leslie Bedford gave Britten a present: a copy of *Nonsense Songs* – settings of texts from *Alice in Wonderland*, composed by his mother, Liza Lehmann. Britten and Pears started calling the Bedfords 'The Two Leslieys' and young Steuart, 'Stewy'.

◊

I MET THEM AS A PAIR. I was six years old when my mother joined the English Opera Group, as it was to become, for *The Rape of Lucretia* in 1946. She was one of the two Lucias. They did everything with two casts. Britten was particularly interested because she had three boys, and all of them were showing signs of musical talent. So it was inevitable, really, that he would become quite friendly with her. They were frequent guests at our house in Hampstead Garden Suburb, and when they came it was always very interesting and great fun.

We played a lot of ping-pong and cricket in the garden, and we would get lots of fiery letters from neighbours complaining about the cricket balls being whacked over the fence into their gardens, as often as not by Ben.

I remember Peter as being very much the one that had a schoolmasterly feel about him. He was a very big man, intimidating. We didn't sort of warm to him in the same way that one warmed to Ben. Ben was wonderfully happy in the company of young people. There was nothing sinister about this at all. He was just happy in their company and if you went to Crag House, their home in Aldeburgh, for instance, there was always something going on: a fascinating jigsaw on the piano or a bit of table tennis going on somewhere else. There was always something like that, something that attracted the young people, and we were very attracted to him and particularly when he started playing the piano.

I was by that stage getting very, very interested in the piano and I was immediately grabbed by the way he played. Instinctively I sort of went for it. It would seem to be quite extraordinary, but everything he did at the keyboard, whatever he played, was something special. It was never just plonked down or he never just ran through something; it was always special. Strangely enough, he never played any of his own pieces. He always played somebody else's and so I wasn't so aware of the compositions, which I should have been really.

There was a time when I had fallen in love with a Bach fugue. Someone had got a record of it but I couldn't find a copy of the music anywhere. In Crag House there was a Bach Gesellschaft, so I persuaded Ben to get it out. It was one in A minor (BWV 947) and I'd heard it arranged for strings on the record. So Ben played it through, and there's a moment in the middle of that fugue where it goes into sixths. It's not written for the keyboard really; it just runs along in sixths. It's quite awkward to play. And I watch Ben's right hand going around in a sort of circular motion. He's sight-reading with absolute perfection without the slightest problem, saying at the same time, 'I don't really like this very much!' But he got to the end.

And then he was very good at doing a Chico Marx impression, and he would do all the glissandos and everything.

With Peter, it wasn't the same thing at all. Although he was fun in a sense. He had this sort of schoolmasterly appearance. There was something that made one hold back. Whereas with Ben one was entirely happy.

The fun with Ben was that he was always ready to enter into the total japes that young people got up to. During the holidays we had a cousin staying with us, John Duff – the same age as my brother David – who was a terrible scape-grace. He got into all sorts of trouble. My father, who was an engineer by profession, once gave us the recipe for making a special sort of potassium chlorate bomb, and this involved mixing potassium chlorate and sugar, which we would wrap up in a tight little ball in something like an old paper bag. And then you clouted it with a hammer and it went off with the most wonderful explosion, really impressive. And we used to do this with great care. We usually had big gloves and would hide behind a wooden box as we'd bang the hammer down, and the bigger the bag the more exciting it was.

So, of course, when Ben and Peter came we had to show them this. We mixed up an especially big one, hoping that there would be an enormous explosion. We took it out onto the front doorstep, at which point we started putting on our protective gear, but Peter just picked up the hammer and just went whack without the slightest care or concern. And there was the most enormous explosion you ever heard. It was tremendous, absolutely wonderful, but he was a bit surprised. Ben was somewhat shocked, and it brought the neighbours out across the street. We'd woken up the children and they all thought some frightful accident had happened, that there'd been a gas explosion or something. So we all slunk back inside the house shamefacedly.

He was always up to something if there were people of our age around. One day we'd all been out and we ended up in Oulton Broad where there was a tea room, as I recall. My father was there too, the three of us, and Ben. The minute we sat down Ben took a knife, put the blade on the edge of the table and held it there while he flicked the handle with his other hand. And it made this extraordinary 'doing-doing-doing' sound, a sort of knife xylophone effect, which he modified by moving the knife around. The minute he started doing it, we were all doing it, and the whole table was making all this noise. The waitress came up, looking rather shocked. Of course, David, who became a composer, incorporated it into one of his compositions.

I went to a very early performance of the *Serenade* in the Jubilee Hall in Aldeburgh with Dennis Brain. For some reason I wasn't as struck by it as I felt I ought to have been. I don't know why. It was later, when I got to know these pieces, I realised what such a wonderful treasury of music there was there.

There was nothing sinister about his attraction to young people. I mean you'd have thought if there was anything like that we would have known. But there was no sort of the inappropriate touching or fondling that people go on about these days at all. We never had anything like that. In my experience, that wasn't part of that relationship at all. I suppose it never really dawned on me that Ben was homosexual until I left school. My parents never talked about it.

I didn't realise what was going on in Ben's and Peter's relationship, that it was illegal as far as British law was concerned. That certainly didn't cross my mind for a long time.

Yoxford, Suffolk, October 2017

Steuart has just dropped a bottle of champagne. The bottle was only half full, so the spillage is meagre, nor has the bottle broken, but a glass he was holding in the same hand has also dropped to the tiled floor and smashed.

'Oh shit, I'm sorry!'

Celia, Steuart's wife, calmly manages the clean-up. She's remarkably unflustered. Her first concern is Steuart.

Steuart has recently been diagnosed with Parkinson's disease. This is the first time I've seen him since he told me about it on the phone a few weeks before, when I also said, 'Oh shit, I'm sorry.'

He had the feeling for a few months that something wasn't right. He was conducting *Albert Herring* – an opera he has conducted many, many times – and kept getting lost or making mistakes when playing the piano during the recitatives. There would be moments of panic when he simply couldn't remember what had just happened on stage or in the pit. It was both terrifying and confusing.

As soon as he had the diagnosis, Steuart put a stop to his career.

He cannot bear to work and make mistakes, despite my protestations that history is littered with elderly conductors who can barely move, let alone tell you the day of the week, who are lauded for merely standing in front of orchestras and wobbling a bit – 'Such mastery! Such insight!' – but Steuart is having none of it.

An uncle of mine – a brilliant biochemist, artist and lover of wine – has recently died after struggling for several years with the same type of Parkinson's. I have an inkling of what's in store. I have seen what the disease does to great minds.

So here we are, at Steuart's and Celia's house in Suffolk, having lunch with a swift glass of champagne before we eat. The dropping of the bottle and the glass is symptomatic, a sudden loss of grip. He has no obvious chorea or shaking, but I can notice him struggling a little to find the right words. And his gait has become a little hunched, his walk slightly shuffling. He is managing the rare act of looking oddly youthful for a man in his late seventies yet frail at the same time.

Celia thinks Steuart should write his autobiography or, more precisely, write a memoir about his life working with Benjamin Britten.

'But he needs some help, and I think I know just the man.' She eyeballs me.

'What? Me?!' I'm very flattered but I have no experience in this sort of thing. I demur. The subject changes and we eat lunch.

A few days later I change my mind. I'm too intrigued. How can I, an enormous Britten fan, pass up the opportunity to sit at Steuart's feet, even if they are clad in socks and sandals, and hear all his stories?

I've known, admired, loved Steuart for thirty-odd years. We've performed five Britten operas together. *War Requiem* too. My wife and I almost bought the house next door to theirs. And in all that time he has never talked about his relationship with the composer. I've seen other singers ask him about Britten – 'What was he like?' – and seen Steuart squirm a little as a result, uncomfortable with the attention, or bamboozled by the complexity and inanity of the question.

So here is my opportunity to find out about the defining relationship of his career and arguably of his life.

The problem is the disease. Can we complete the book in time, before Steuart's memory is too deeply locked within him?

TWO

A thirst, a leaping, wild unrest, a deep desire

In the spring of 1947, Lesley Duff was cast in Britten's next opera, *Albert Herring*, as the adolescent schoolgirl Emmie. It isn't a demanding singing role, so for Duff's self-confidence it didn't present the same problems as *Lucretia*. The cast met for the first playthrough at Pears's flat in Oxford Square:

> Ben was again excited and tense but there was a degree of light-heartedness and ease that had not been there on the previous 'preview' of *Lucretia*. He was among trusted friends and, more important still, he was away from the atmosphere of self-opinionated intolerance, of wealth and the sort of power that wealth gives, that was Glyndebourne. That atmosphere was sheer poison to Ben.

John Christie, Glyndebourne's owner, had underwritten the previous year's tour of *Lucretia* and lost a lot of money, which had soured forever an already difficult relationship with Britten. Christie's appetite was for Mozart and Strauss. He would say of *Herring* to an audience member, 'This isn't *our* kind of thing, you know.' No longer under the aegis of the Glyndebourne Opera Company, Britten had his own English Opera Group. They would still perform one short season at Glyndebourne, giving both *Lucretia* and *Herring*, but as an independent company.

Britten's playthroughs were an experience shared by Duff and, later, by Steuart. The *Herring* playthrough was one of the few experiences of her working life she related to her son, giving him a rare anecdote from 1947:

On some occasions, when he felt pressured by the number of people present, the fast tempos could be somewhat faster than really intended. This happened once in the early days of *Albert Herring*, when Ben was so keyed up that the velocity became almost preposterous. Fortunately, Margaret Ritchie was on hand to defuse the situation. 'Ben, my dear, can't we have it a bit *faster*?'

Duff was becoming closer to Britten's inner circle. Britten and Pears were the frequent recipients of acrimonious letters from people who disapproved of their lifestyle as much as they hated Britten's music, and Duff was at Oxford Square one day when a letter arrived.

Ben came into the room holding it as if he had a poisonous snake by the tail, with a face like a sheet.

'What is it?' said Peter quickly.

'It's this letter,' said Ben, growing whiter and more tortured-looking. 'It's pretty beastly.'

Longing to say anything to comfort that sick look, I said, 'A letter like that can't hurt *you*, Ben. It can only hurt the writer.'

'No,' he said. 'It can't hurt me, can it? It *can't* hurt my music.'

The continual criticism and misjudging, and the endless hostility and jeers that he had had to face through the war and through his love for Peter had caused him such agony that I doubt if his approach to people, or to life, can ever be free now from fear or bitterness. I wonder whether this will always be heard in his music.

He endured a considerable amount of castigation, not only for his sexuality but for his pacifist views. He had to put up with an enormous amount of opprobrium. The BBC was getting very upset, asking, 'Should we be using this composer?' While he had been in the USA in 1941 with his absence attracting hostility in the UK, Britten had actually asked his publishers not to promote performances of his works. Many people took a very strong line, bearing in mind 'living in sin', as it were, with Peter was an affront to the Establishment in those early post-war years.

On another occasion at Oxford Square, Duff rehearsed with the boy singing Harry:

> We all sprawled on the floor trying to prove to Ben that it was impossible to bounce a ball accurately, sing, and watch his beat at the same time. 'I've proved it,' he said. 'I have spent *hours* proving it.'

Britten's fastidious attention to the detail of bouncing the ball in time is a trait that most singers who have ever worked with Steuart will probably recognise.

While *Herring* was in rehearsal at Glyndebourne, *Lucretia* was being revived with a few cast changes from the year before. A last-minute emergency was to challenge Duff's self-confidence again:

> *Lucretia* was left without a Lucia when Irene Elsinger left the cast four days before the first performance. [Elizabeth Parry took over the role.] I was not asked to take up my Lucia again and in a sudden shock of pain I realised it simply hadn't been good enough. More, that perhaps it had been so bad that Ben could not bear to hear it again from me. I was determined not to show any sign, but Ben waylaid me behind the stage.
> 'Why are you unhappy?' he said abruptly.
> It threw me badly off my balance.
> 'Because I'm not good enough for you,' I said finally. 'My God, since when?'
> 'Always, I think, but I'm only just sure of it.'
> 'Why, why suddenly? You're singing beautifully.'

I could only shake my head desperately. Then he put his arms around me and said, 'I can't have you unhappy. I simply *can't*. I won't let you go till you say you're happy.'

How like a child, that suddenly cannot bear to see the hurt he has almost unwittingly inflicted.

The next night he called me to his room. 'I've got something for you,' he said. 'They have just come and I am awfully proud of them.' And there was the first copy of the *Donne Sonnets* to be given away. And to me. 'For my dearest Lesley,' he wrote, 'with love and admiration.'

I put my arms around him and said, 'Oh Ben, I *am* a beast. Please forgive me.'

'You're a darling,' he said.

In Oxford Square a few weeks later, Britten persuaded Duff to sing through Lucia for him, to see if he could put her mind at rest. He had revised the opera in the course of 1946 and 1947, including some changes for Lucia:

I sang the flower scene and then started on the first act. Ben was playing superbly for me, now and then sending me a sweet encouraging smile. I stumbled over the Lucia. Peter, tense and angry beyond any reason, threw a cushion madly across the room and flung out, 'It's all right, darling!'

Ben whispered to me, 'I'm on your side', and every bit of his will was concentrated on helping me.

They got me through it, and Ben told me he wanted me to take up the part again.

I think my mother's difficulty with Lucia lay in the fact she was actually a heavier singer than the soubrette the part really needs. She wasn't happy 'floating' her voice, and that made it rather difficult. The section that made her the unhappiest was the Linen Trio. They were so far upstage that they couldn't hear the orchestra and nearly always ended up a semitone flat. It must have been excruciating, for her and for Ben. Hence her describing *Lucretia* as the 'most ill-served piece'.

The English Opera Group took *Herring* on tour that summer. In Scheveningen, in the Netherlands, Duff describes a hot evening:

Ben was eating an ice very slowly and with the intense concentration of a small boy.

'Just look at Ben's technique with an ice!' said Joan Cross.

'He looks like all my small boys rolled into one,' I said. 'That's why I love him.'

After a short break back in England, the English Opera Group was in Lucerne, Switzerland:

An atmosphere almost joyous in its relaxation, the heat made tolerable by the wonderful colours from the lake and mountains.

We spent Sunday morning on the lake. Nancy Evans and I rowed. Ben appeared to be deeply alarmed at the receding coast, so he ordered us to get back at once, which we found more easily said than done as the boat, extraordinarily ill-balanced, went round in circles and the shore, after considerable effort, was further than ever. I think he was really nervous and distressed at our lack of concern.

'Peter, for heaven's sake, you and Lesley side by side . . . Is that any way to trim a boat?!' We had to make a determined effort to pull nearer in, where he immediately relaxed, and we bathed and rowed and bathed again, and the beloved mountains shimmered and leapt in the heat. How happy and well and young he looked in the smallest pair of shorts I have ever seen.

'I think they've shrunk,' he said, pulling at them helplessly.

Pears, Britten, Lesley Duff and Nancy Evans in the garden of Hotel Friedheim, Hergiswil, during the Lucerne tour, August 1947.

We climbed Pilatus. That is, we went up in the funicular and walked down; up through the pines and the waterfalls, out onto the bare rock above the tree level, with Lucerne dropping away below us.

He sat remote and quiet, suddenly rapt. He was working out some quartet that was looming in his mind, and he stayed utterly still. Then he came up to me as I leaned on the parapet looking a hundred miles away to the Jungfrau. He said no words but stood holding me very tightly.

We determined to make a fairly quick descent as the darkness was not far away, so Peter, Ben and I started on the track down. Then Ben, letting out a yell, proceeded to tear down the path, cutting off the corners, closely followed by myself and then Peter. A madness was in us all, that clean, true, glorious mountain madness. We ran together and then quietened and dropped down hour after hour, talking of beliefs, of faults, of our childhood, of many other things. Peter was quiet, Ben full of ideas and gaiety, and eventually we reached the sloping fields above the village.

We left Hergiswil, and two days later we broadcast from Zurich and said goodbye. I took the plane from Zurich. I left them to come in more leisurely fashion by road and boat.

On his return to Aldeburgh, Britten moved into his new home, Crag House, on Crabbe Street, which he had bought in June. It was time for a holiday before the EOG resumed touring for the autumn. The Bedfords rented a house on the Norfolk Broads and Britten joined the family for a few days:

Ben came to us to sail on the Broads. To have him in my home – one with the children, casual, carefree, a little shy – after our relationship of composer-conductor, supreme authority, and very humble member of the cast – was odd, to say the least of it. I felt it was the beginning of something really rather lovely and lasting, and was deeply happy to see his affection for the children develop and his shyness with Leslie drop away. I saw him as his most real self – quite lost in a game of cricket where every other ball went into the Broad and had to be salvaged with sticks and abstruse calculations as to current and tide. Comical balls to Steuart until he was doubled up with laughter. Taking the boat out in half a gale and coming back exhausted and intensely happy with water over their ankles.

The conditions were undeniably primitive and I was suddenly struck with the absurdity of this Darling of the Gods, used to every luxury, having to draw water from the Broad in a bucket to wash with. I said as much and he answered with utter sincerity, 'Don't you know, this is what I *really* love? How often I have to make myself do what I hate, and meet people I don't want? It's heaven to be able to be just myself.'

They were deeply happy days, but I was conscious of a lingering shyness at being in our home. The three days cemented a growing trust between him and the boys, which is a very lovely thing in their lives and I believe a precious thing in his.

Britten's visit to the Bedfords on the Norfolk Broads lasted only two days in early September of 1947. Pears didn't come, but Britten wrote to him about his trip:

> I'm writing this scribble because it's so difficult to phone at that house – small room, smell of cooking, & people over-hearing. But all the same I'll telephone when I get back from the Broads to see how you are & tell you about it all!

Steuart remembers the house they had rented as being very basic, a bungalow, its chief appeal for his father being the dinghy that was moored alongside. It was in this boat that the enthusiastic but unskilled Leslie took his family sailing and they would end up stuck in the mud. It was around this time that Britten drew a picture for Steuart:

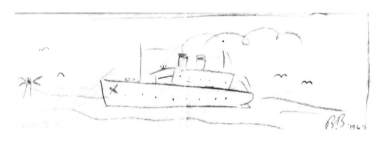

Shortly after the Norfolk holiday, Steuart was sent away to join his brother David at Hillsbrow Preparatory School in Redhill, on the opposite side of London. Now he would see his parents only during the holidays and on occasional weekend visits. With all three boys away at school, touring was less complicated for Lesley. She no longer needed to drive late at night to get home. And she was free to spend time with her new friends, Ben and Peter, whenever she was invited.

Lucretia was touring again, this time with Stanford Robinson conducting and some major cast changes. By the time it came to London for some performances at Covent Garden, morale in the company was low:

The first London night was an appalling artistic failure. Ben's behaviour was an example of selflessness that I have never seen him equal. The evening must have been one of utter horror to him, but never by look, or by word or gesture, did he let *us* as the cast have the slightest suspicion that he wasn't completely satisfied.

The production moved on to Bournemouth and again Duff found herself in difficulties with the tessitura of her role, Lucia. Britten made some cuts and changes, but these compounded her sense of failure. He did his best to reassure her, waiting in the wings for her to finish her Achilles heel, the Linen Scene, and throwing her a kiss and flashing a smile. At the interval he was in her dressing room.

'I'm so glad,' he said with his arms around me. 'That's *that* bogey properly laid!'

The week finished with him conducting us. We had a wonderful rehearsal with him. *Lucretia* suddenly sprang to life – every phrase that had become distorted and meaningless he put into shape and explained and lit up with his imagination.

'Don't worry tonight,' he said. 'It can only be a sort of mad rehearsal. You can never remember all these things but let's enjoy it!'

The tour continued to Oxford. One day, Duff drove Britten to rehearsals for *Peter Grimes* at Covent Garden. He wasn't happy with the cast:

Poor Ben. Here was money in abundance, the pick of the artistic world, the finest orchestra and conductor, and no idea even of how to learn the words correctly. The suffering was very intense for him and he looked very ill as we drove back to Oxford.

Through the following autumn I saw him on one or two particularly happy occasions. The first was his birthday. I was very surprised and very touched at being invited. They played us their latest records – Purcell's *The Queen's Epicedium*. Ben watched me while it was being played and got up and put his arms around me. How does he know the secrets of my heart without a word or a look being exchanged?

There was another night later in the year when they were broadcasting and I went to the studio. The broadcast was a great success and they were in roaring spirits. I drove them home, Ben talking in unspeakable German, in deference, he said, to a Swiss guest also in the car with us. The high spirits and the need for mad, demonstrable affection continued through supper. Then suddenly he was a small boy, very tired and nearly asleep at the table.

Young Steuart was now writing to Britten from his prep school. His letters have not survived but on 4 December 1947, Britten wrote back to Steuart:

Thank you for your nice letters – I loved having them. I am staying in Ireland for a few days and having a lovely time – but the boat we came on rocked terribly. I wasn't sea sick tho'. How are you?
Love from Ben

At some time towards the end of the year, Anne Wood, the general manager of the English Opera Group, and not Britten himself, told Duff that she wouldn't be rehired to sing Lucia or Emmie. She was sacked. Professionally, it was a devastating blow. Personally, she seems to have been able to be more objective. As long as she could be of some use to Ben, to adore him, to chauffeur him in her little car, everything was still all right. And as long as someone other than Britten himself did the sacking (even though she knew perfectly well who was calling the shots) she could keep the professional and the personal separate.

At Christmas, there was an exchange of presents. Lesley gave Britten a painting by her father R. K. Duff, *Sheep in a Meadow*, and a book by

Above 'Stewy', *c.* 1944, beginning his life-long love of biscuits.
Below Steuart (centre), aged twelve, captain of Hillsbrow cricket team, 1952.

Members of the English Opera Group during the European tour in 1947: *left to right* Benjamin Britten, Peter Pears, Joan Cross, Otakar Kraus and Lesley Duff.

Family snapshots of Leslie, David and Peter Bedford, part of a collage Lesley kept at her bedside towards the end of her life.

The Rape of Lucretia (1946): Lesley Duff (Lucia) and Nancy Evans (Lucretia). Lesley Duff referred to the opera as 'the most ill-served piece'.

Albert Herring (1947): Peter Pears (Albert) with Lesley Duff (Emmie), David Spenser (Harry) and Anne Sharp (Cissie). John Christie commented, 'This isn't *our* kind of thing, you know.'

Steuart Bedford, c. 1970.

the seventeenth-century physician and philosopher Sir Thomas Browne, who spent most of his life in Norwich. Ben – who had just started work on the cantata *Saint Nicolas* at the time – sent a package to Lesley with this note:

What a lovely book – thank you so *very* much for it. A lovely period of people and a charming example is Sir TB. You do choose beautifully! The enclosed book is for the boys. Sorry I couldn't get presents separately, but Nicolas takes all my time! Giv'em my love and say I'll find a way *somehow* of playing them ping-pong.

Your father's sheep look lovely on our wall here – I like it a whole heap.

As 1947 ended, Britten sent Duff a card:

Is lunch and ping-pong alright for your family on Saturday?

Lesley recorded the occasion:

Only 24 hours in London but he had promised the children and a promise to children was inviolable. I sensed something unhappy and wrong when he arrived, that he knew he ought to speak to me about the opera. In the end I gave him his opening and we had a very moving and revealing conversation.

They had practically nothing to offer but would offer [any role] on condition that I felt in no way bound to do it for any reason whatever of loyalty or ties of affection. That was the gist of it. But how he knew my desperate sense of failure and loss and emptiness, and how he tried with every bit of understanding and affection at his command to put it right, as if it mattered and mattered supremely.

◊

IT'S CLEAR SHE LOVED BEN, absolutely. She realised his talent almost immediately, that he was a perfectionist, like her. He got upset very easily. But the thing that struck me as very curious is what the other members of the company must have thought. Because in an opera company it's something that everybody talks about. Nobody seemed to mind the fact that Ben spent a lot of time with Lesley. She acted almost as a sort of secretary. She was always driving him, from Cambridge to London for instance, or down to Aldeburgh. But it didn't seem to bother anybody. Nowadays that sort of thing would be remarked on almost immediately.

Like my mother, I've always been a perfectionist and sometimes it gets in your way.

But there's no question about it, she was totally in love with Ben, with everything that Ben did. It was just wonderful. Which I can understand.

◊

Gosforth, Newcastle-upon-Tyne, August 1996

The church is being set up for the first of several recording sessions. At the altar end, there is a low platform for the singers, and in the body of the church, chairs and music stands laid out for the chamber orchestra.

The recording is of *Albert Herring*. Steuart is conducting. But before he conducts and well before the cast and orchestra arrive, he is busy moving chairs, adjusting music stands, and arranging where he wants the players. In the centre of the circle of players' chairs is a grand piano, which Steuart will play during the opera's recitatives.

From a plastic carrier bag – Steuart's favoured means of carrying scores, books, pencils, batons, sandwiches, etc. – he pulls out an arched plastic object, shaped somewhat like a question mark. It looks familiar, but out of place. I've seen something similar before, but I'm struggling to place where exactly. Then it dawns on me. I've seen this thing on the back of a washing machine. It's to support the drain hose and make sure it doesn't kink. What on earth is Steuart going to do with that?

He digs around in his plastic carrier bag and pulls out a clamp. Using the clamp, he carefully fastens the bottom of the plastic gizmo, the washing-machine-hose de-kinker, to the bottom end of the piano's key-board. He digs in the carrier bag again and produces a small bell and some parcel tape. He fixes the bell to the top end of the plastic gizmo with the tape, making sure that the bell is secure but will still ring freely. It does.

But what is he going to do with this Heath Robinson contraption that is now fixed to the grand piano? He sits down at the piano, plays a phrase from the opera, flings out his left hand and slaps the bell. Now I get it. Now it makes sense.

It's the bell on the door of the Herring grocery shop that rings whenever anyone enters or leaves. The ring of the bell is marked clearly in the score. And Steuart being Steuart, the inventor's son, the firm believer that if you want to get something done, you should probably do it yourself, has devised his own solution to something that, probably, no one else had foreseen might even be a problem. Yet it could have become a terrible problem that would waste hours of expensive recording time.

The solution is just so, well, Steuart.

But there are questions that still have to be asked. Where did he get the washing-machine-hose de-kinker from? His own machine at home (which he will have definitely plumbed in himself)? Almost certainly. In that case, does his machine not need one? Possibly not – they're not always essential – but if it does, it is hard not to visualise the machine at home, stripped of its part, spewing foaming suds onto the kitchen floor. And if it's not needed, at what point did Steuart think to himself, 'I don't need the washing-machine-hose de-kinker, but I'd better not get rid of it because – you never know – it could come in handy one day'?

In that case, I like to think that Steuart's sense of satisfaction on finding a useful function for the washing-machine-hose de-kinker was absolutely and utterly immense.

THREE

Should I give up the fruitless struggle with the word?

Britten's new work for the English Opera Group in 1948 was his reworking of John Gay's *The Beggar's Opera*. The only role on offer to Lesley Duff was in the ensemble, where she also had one solo line as Mrs Vixen. Whatever qualms she must have had about this step down from being a main cast member she kept to herself. Clearly she was willing to overcome them in order to stay in Britten's orbit. Besides, she could now work for him and be relieved of the self-destructive angst that she was consistently failing to meet his standards – and hers, for that matter. Putting on *The Beggar's Opera* was a more relaxed experience for Britten too – initially at least – because his stake in it was also less.

One day Ben rang up. 'Can your boys give me some cricket tomorrow?' he said. 'I've got my only free afternoon in six months.'

So I fetched him and saw again the lovely relaxation of youth spring up in his face and the happy ease that is always his with children.

'Come for a walk with us,' he said, when every ball the house possessed had been batted into oblivion in the neighbouring gardens. We went across Hampstead Heath and over to Kenwood where the rhododendrons were just budding. We talked about the children. He felt that one should not be too violent in sharing our beliefs with our children, or in influencing them to share those beliefs. They must be part of their own world as they grow up and any obvious deviation from it was going to cause a great deal of suffering. Only can one *be* the things one believes, surround them with the almost unspoken atmosphere of those things and watch with patience how their spirits react to it or seek out their own way.

We passed through Kenwood, back onto the windy heath, and with deep love he spoke of Peter's work, his joy with the fact that he would come to Aldeburgh and have his own room there and be with him. 'Nothing makes sense unless you are with the one you love.'

'Ben,' I said, 'do you believe that if you want a perfection strongly enough and work hard enough, in the end and with infinite patience you will find it?'

'No,' he said. 'I don't think I do. Not quite like that. But when I wake in the night I know that my work is not really good, all I hope for. All I am concerned for is that somehow I may have laid a bridge for those that are coming, or in some way shown the way to a greater perfection, though I shall not have got near it myself. You know, too much success is just as bad for a man as too much failure. Either is extremely uncomfortable.'

I drove him over to dinner with a friend – a friend to whom he had been very close in the past, whose friendship had been broken by the friend's wife – this was to be their first meeting since the quarrel and he began to get rather tense and white. 'I hate rudeness, it makes me feel severely ill,' he said.

They rehearsed in the old Festival Theatre on the outskirts of Cambridge, once a fine Victorian theatre but now a squalid scenery store for the newer Arts Theatre, where the opera was to have its premiere. Clearly infatuated but still insecure about their friendship, Duff decided her best policy was to be professional and distant, and she barely spoke to Britten. Though she did ask him one day what it was that put him off people 'so violently':

'Almost anything, at any time, I'm afraid.'

I was determined somehow to walk the tightrope of friendship till some indestructible stability had been found.

Once the opera opened she was soon useful again, driving Britten back and forth to London:

I picked Ben up outside Covent Garden. He came out very tired, nervy, wrought up into a depressed tensity by the rehearsal of *Grimes* he had just been watching.

Richard Lewis was singing the title role:

'I simply can't bear it. He's such a nice boy but I can't bear to hear him do it.'

He relaxed a little as we swung round into Oxford Street, going by the Berners Hotel and heading for Boosey's, where he had to fetch music. We turned onto the Great North Road, talking of Guthrie, and Eric and Nancy and various trivial happy commonplaces.

Tyrone Guthrie was directing *The Beggar's Opera*, in which the mezzo-soprano Nancy Evans was cast as Polly Peachum. At Glyndebourne she had sung Lucretia as well as Nancy in *Albert Herring*. She was to marry Eric Crozier in 1949, a second marriage for them both. Crozier had directed the first productions of *Peter Grimes* at Sadler's Wells and *The Rape of Lucretia* at Glyndebourne. He wrote the libretto for *Albert Herring* and the text for *Saint Nicolas*.

Just past the Barn on the Barnet bypass we stopped for tea. I had a thermos and a tin of gingerbread for him. Somehow, the conversation got onto his composing. I very hesitatingly said, 'Of all you have written, Ben, the Canticle [*My Beloved is Mine*] is my first beloved.' He turned to me in the car with a very gentle smile and said very quietly, 'You are a clever girl. It's *much* my best piece.'

So we drove on. In Stevenage he said, 'Where was the garage Peter phoned me from when he went off with the key of the Rolls?'

I was surprised in the moment for I did not begin then to know all the angles, the differing facets, the height and depth and terrible intensity of his love for Peter, and this struck me as so oddly revealing that I was surprised that he had said it to me.

I said, 'It's up that road. Shall we go up? It's not that far.'

'No,' he said, 'but it's nice somehow to know.'

I think this was a glimmer of the torture that was his love for Peter. How has it been possible for this intensely sensitive creature to bear the insults and the written and spoken sneers without having been twisted near insanity?

As we came into the suburbs of Cambridge he touched on a personal trouble of mine that I had confided to him, with great gentleness and understanding. 'If I can ever help . . .'

We got to the stage door, the end of our drive, and my birthday, and Peter coming to me with a beautiful old jug from him and Ben.

'Did you know you had given me a present, Ben?' I said.

'No,' he said, 'but I hoped I had!'

It isn't clear what had happened in Stevenage in the fairly recent past. Pears had driven off – from London perhaps, or from Cambridge during the *Beggar's Opera* rehearsals – presumably in his own car and taking with him the keys to Britten's car, the Rolls. Britten's and Pears's relationship was quite rocky during the late 1940s; Lesley Duff was witness to at least one major row between them. This might well have been the aftermath of another.

The most likely explanation seems to be that Pears, in a huff for some reason, drove off, taking Britten's car keys with him, possibly out of pettiness or possibly to stop Britten following him. Pears pulled into a garage in

Stevenage, rang Britten to say he was leaving the keys at the garage – possibly they had had a further heated argument on the phone – and he drove on. At Britten's request, Lesley must have driven to the garage to pick up the keys. It is also possible that Pears had accidentally driven off with Britten's car keys in his pocket, realised, and stopped at Stevenage to ring and tell him. But this scenario doesn't seem to merit the emotional significance that Britten attaches to the event, nor does it make much sense alongside Lesley's description of the 'torture' of their relationship. In either scenario, it is clear it was Lesley who had to drive to Stevenage to pick up the car keys.

◊

I THINK A VERY INTERESTING question to ask is what would have happened to Peter if he had not met Ben? Would he have had a similar career? And that's a very difficult question to answer because Ben did so much for Peter. Literally put him on the map in many ways. Not just by writing those things for him but by accompanying him in recitals, which must have been a very uplifting experience for anybody. Was Peter always going to be the great artist that he became? Would he have become a great artist if Ben hadn't been in the background, and did Peter actually know that?

The dynamics of that relationship have never been fathomed. It was a very intriguing relationship and I never quite knew what was going on.

There are all sorts of theories bandied about that Ben's serious illnesses always came in the wake of some total bust-up with Peter. I don't know whether this is true or not.

The illnesses and injuries were in a sense psychosomatic. That elbow that went on him, which meant he couldn't conduct, was almost certainly self-inflicted, I feel. And of course his stomach was notoriously tender. He had to be very careful what he ate because it would blow up at the slightest provocation. Whereas Peter could eat anything, absolutely anything at all. He could eat rock and it wouldn't make the slightest difference.

He said to me once, 'The only thing I don't like is seedy cake.' Everything else he would devour, every time, no problem.

The other thing one has to accept, the unfortunate truth, is that poor old Peter was – how can I put this? – he was sexually quite alive. Ben was perfectly happy about this as long as he didn't know about it, he always used to say. And Peter did have affairs with other people, particularly when he was abroad. This was all part of the package as to what Peter was like. Although he was devoted to Ben – there's no doubt about that – I think the greater devotion was from Ben to Peter. Ben was, of course, much more buttoned up emotionally. Because of his sort of Victorian upbringing, you might say, he kept himself very well in check. He wouldn't have allowed himself to get involved in some sort of affair with somebody else, I'm quite sure. That's my opinion, I have to say. I don't state that as a fact.

◊

During the run of *The Beggar's Opera*, just before that year's Aldeburgh Festival, Lesley Duff joined Britten, Pears, Eric Crozier and Nancy Evans for a short holiday in Aldeburgh:

We all piled into the Little Biscuit [Lesley's nickname for her BSA car] and drove to Southwold, climbing up the cliffs at Dunwich, the wind in our faces and the salt on our lips. We had tea in a little cafe and looked at bookshops where Ben bought me a copy of Marcus [Aurelius]. We walked by the sea that night. It was stormy and the waves were crashing on the shingle. Every few moments there was a stillness in the sky and the moon swung through the tatter of clouds, or a star gave sudden hope.

'I've got to tell you something, Ben. You've got something wrong about me.'

He turned and gave me his whole attention. 'Dear Lesley,' he said, 'you don't need to explain any more. I may be a fool, but I am not quite such a fool as not to know what these three years have been to you.' I was gripped with a fear that he knew too much of the intensity of my feelings and was perhaps a little bored by it.

'Is it all right?' And after a very quiet moment he answered, 'It's quite all right.'

'Oh Ben, I'm so glad of you,' I said, and he holding my hands in both of his, said, 'Do you know what knowing you has given to Peter and to me?'

And his arms were tightly round me and his strong love reassuring me, all I could say was 'God bless you, Ben. Good night.'

The final picture of the [Aldeburgh] Festival that remains with me is Ben at the head of a procession of small boys – rather dirty and dishevelled small boys – entering the very exclusive premises of the Slaughden Yacht Club, sitting them down to a royal tea and waiting on them as his honoured guests.

We went to Cambridge for the [Cambridge] Festival. A heat wave was on us, and I think it was during that week that Ben really began to feel the approach of the illness that was to grow on him that summer and end by defeating him. *Saint Nicolas* was performed in King's Chapel. Afterwards he said to me hesitatingly, 'I think it made sense, didn't it?'

'Ben, it made such sense that I shall remember it, think of it, when I am dying.'

He held my hand tightly and said, 'Oh, dear Lesley.'

Lennox Berkeley's *Stabat Mater* was given a performance, memorable because Ben was attacked by quite uncontrollable giggles in the moment of raising his baton, by a peculiar squeak coming from the cello.

The week's schedule in Cambridge was punishing for Britten and Pears. There were four performances of *Albert Herring* at the Arts Theatre in which Britten shared the conducting with Ivan Clayton, and Pears alternated the title role with Richard Lewis. There were also two orchestral concerts featuring Britten and Pears, the second the performance of *Saint Nicolas* that Duff describes. To finish the week they performed *The Beggar's Opera* in concert, followed by a Schubert recital the next day.

> I remember the heat of that afternoon and Ben's light-headedness, and then his haggard look after the interval. It was soon explained. A laughing crowd of us round the stage door and Gladys Parr [who took the spoken role of the Beggar] saying, 'Give me an autograph, Mr Britten!' and Ben's look of sudden pain as he said, 'You wouldn't want it if you had read what I read about myself in the *Telegraph*. Unfortunately, I read it in the interval and it made me sick!' Poor, dear Ben.
>
> Then the long drive back to London with Peter beside me and Ben and Eric in the back, Ben terribly quiet and feeling very ill and reticent.

In mid-August, the Bedford family returned to the Norfolk Broads for their summer holiday. Lesley seems to have gone ahead on her own, and Britten joined her for a few days before the arrival of Leslie, and Steuart and his older brothers. Then he joined them again a week later, when he also brought the fourteen-year-old Humphrey Maud, one of the dedicatees of *The Young Person's Guide to the Orchestra*, the son of the senior civil servant John Redcliffe-Maud and his pianist wife Jean Hamilton. This would be the family's last holiday on the Broads. The Bedfords had decided to buy a holiday cottage in Snape from Lesley's fellow Lucia in *The Rape of Lucretia*, Margaret Ritchie, and they moved in during late August. Britten wrote to Lesley from Aldeburgh ahead of the visit:

> Humphrey is arriving here midday Saturday & we plan to drive up to you in the afternoon, if you'll tell us that that's all right! We

could make it later, Sunday, perhaps if it's best for you. We'll have to come back on Tuesday, because visitors arrive then! Can't say how much we're looking forward to it. (If you could write & tell me (remind me!) exactly when we come too it might save delay!)

Barbara [Parker, Britten's housekeeper] tells me to tell you that the tenants are clearing out of cottage no. 2 now, so it's all yours when you want. Perhaps you'll come over (with family) to see & plan when you're on the Broads!

Excuse haste – just off to Ipswich. We're having a lovely time doing *nothing* – love from Peter (beautifully relaxed), Kathleen F. (ditto), Bartons & lots from me, to you all.

The Aldeburgh gathering included the contralto Kathleen Ferrier – the other Lucretia at Glyndebourne – and Britten's schoolfriend Francis Barton and his family. Lesley recounts the holiday in some detail:

There are pictures I have of him during the few days he stayed with us on the Broads. Drying up for me with infinite care and saying casually as he put the plates down, 'I am so glad you've taken the cottage. We shall need the people we love close to us in the years that are coming.'

A hysterical night when someone tried to break into the bungalow and I rushed into his room. I think we were both rather scared but would have died sooner than admit it. So we laughed instead and couldn't find the light switches and fell over chairs and tables, Ben begging to make me tea or anything in the nature of a sedative, and finally insisting on sleeping with his door and mine open for mutual comfort.

Ben sailing in a tough breeze, his hair on end and his eyes alight, coming back to lie on the veranda, tired, and lying while the sky filled with stillness and birds dived into the marsh, black against the sunset.

'I am sorry I seem far away,' he said one day as we walked along Oulton main street. 'I did want to be free for just enjoying myself but I am working something out and it's like having a baby. You can't help it; you can't put it off.'

And so the days went by, with the children's love immeasurably strengthened for him and his for them. Do they give him perhaps a quality of absolute and undemanding adoration that he cannot find anywhere else? Does it comfort him in some inner loss or hurt? I could see that he, so surrounded by affection of all sorts, from near worship to good brave friendship, should need so desperately this quality of child love.

Lesley remembers two instances that reveal the relationship between Britten and her young sons:

Two incidents stand out for me: Ben coming up to conduct *Albert*, the third act, having heard that my David was in the stalls, as he took his place on the rostrum, searched the rows till he found the little figure there seated, and winked. The composer and conductor on whom the entire performance depended and for whom the packed house behind him was waiting, was looking for a little boy of ten to give happiness to.

And another occasion, during a black week of broadcasts when Ben's illness was gaining on him and the sounds that came through the microphone tortured him, he turned to me and said, 'Would it put you out awfully if I came and saw your boys after the rehearsal? I must have some normal, happy conversation.' So he came, and walking into the house white and ill and tormented, he found the boys playing cricket. In half an hour he was transformed. The lovely look of peace and sanity was there. He was laughing, bowling freak balls to put them off, swinging Steuart over his shoulder, normal, real, sweet. Saved for a little longer to face the nightmares that were gaining on him, of illness, of a loss of Peter, of twisted tormented music that should be the soul of loveliness.

Britten was suffering from a mixture of exhaustion, depression and digestive problems, including a suspected ulcer.

Clearly it was no secret that he lived in fear of Pears leaving him. It isn't hard to imagine what might have been going through Lesley's mind; perhaps she even fantasised that, with Pears gone, she and her boys could become Britten's surrogate family:

Now he seemed to swing into a tide of unhappiness that I, who could only watch and hope, felt might carry him to real disaster. It was mostly, as we learned later, his illness, but it was as if he could find no comfort in anything. The rehearsals were torture, the season at Sadler's Wells, which was such a popular success, was to him a hell of horror. He was distraught over the poor performances of *Albert* and Peter not taking his original part. He drank far too heavily and the resulting illness only made his mental condition worse.

I was taking them home after performances. He would fall into the back of the car (if Peter was there he always made him sit with me) saying, 'Dear, dear faithful Lesley', and torture himself with all that had gone wrong. 'It's not my music, you see,' he would say. 'What causes this disintegration in a company? Why do these mistakes happen?'

'Because they don't care,' I said,

'Oh, I think they do,' said Peter.

Then something mad and bitter tore into my heart and I said uncontrollably, 'They don't know *how* to care. They go away without their scores. They boast they know it so well they can't be bothered. They are *proud* of it. Is that caring?' Ben put his hand on my shoulder and held me a moment.

'Steady,' he said. 'Yes, they care, but only because of hurting me or of their own loss of musical prestige, or that they've let themselves down. They don't care because it's the sin against the Holy Ghost they have committed.'

The next night, a child, he got into the car and, curling close to me, put his head down on my shoulder with an utter hopelessness. I let my hand stroke his head and I said, 'Tired, darling?' How dearly he lay in my heart as my own children was a truth I had almost been afraid to acknowledge to myself.

I went to a dress rehearsal of Ben's version of *The Beggar's Opera* when they brought it to London, but I got scared, I think. I was very young. I got very scared by Otakar Kraus [Lockit, the gaoler] shouting. That sort of slightly overwhelmed me. He was making a terrific noise on stage, bawling about everything and I was just scared as one is sometimes when one's young and something like that happens.

Lesley recalled the inevitable confrontation:

One day he assembled us on the stage – and how many drinks I wonder had he had before he could face this agonising ordeal. He sat on a bench with his arms on the trestle table among the mugs and bits of broken glass. To handle a cast of singers, each one with their own personal prides and prejudices, to tell them they were giving bad work, and yet to keep their loyalty and ensure a good performance for that night was an almost impossible task. And yet with simplicity and sweetness he put over exactly what he wanted.

'I know it's mostly my fault. I am a bad conductor and must often mislead you. I know I do the orchestra, but there's a carelessness getting in and I am blaming no one person for any special mistakes. We stand or fall by the perfection of our work and our attention to detail. I don't want to lecture you – I am as much at fault as you – only to remind you of these little things.' He looked incredibly young. I know he was feeling very sick.

Then Eric Crozier stepped forward and said, 'How can you *expect* good performances when you get your artists so strung up they can hardly face a performance?'

I don't know whether Eric expected the support of the company in this attack. He didn't get any. The company closed their ranks against him quite visibly, and Ben sat, very still, and said quietly, turning to us, 'I hope that's not true. Is this fear among you? Am I making it impossible for you?' He got up and left the stage.

Afterwards he said to me, 'There isn't any truth in that, is there? I am sure I encourage people, even when they don't deserve it.'

This is where Lesley Duff's memoir ends, in early October 1948. There were more performances of *The Beggar's Opera* later in the month, at the People's Palace in East London, and then Lesley had surgery to remove a lump in her neck. Steuart doesn't know what the lump was – it was probably benign – but this could well have been a factor in her struggle with her singing. She gave no more performances with the English Opera Group.

Snape Maltings, 1992

For a singer of my background and sensibilities, this is a big moment: my first professional job at the Aldeburgh Festival. I did sing in the Festival in 1979, when I was in the cast of a version of *Alice in Wonderland* that was brought in from Cambridge, but I was just a student at the time.

This is a different thing altogether. We are recording *The Beggar's Opera* just before we open the Festival with a concert performance. Steuart is conducting a starry line-up that includes Philip Langridge, Ann Murray, Yvonne Kenny and Robert Lloyd. As Filch, I have one song and a bit of dialogue.

I'm on a bit of a roll with Steuart. In the last year, under his baton, I've sung

Flute in *A Midsummer Night's Dream*, The Glass Seller in *Death in Venice*, and now this. The common experience is his meticulous attention to details in the score. He knows every accent, every dynamic, and almost certainly all of them by heart. Volume is not merely loud or soft; there is a marked difference between *mezzo-forte* and *mezzo-piano*, between *piano* and *pianissimo*. These distinctions are extremely important – they are in the score and they cannot be ignored. They balance the sound and texture of the piece, and heaven help you if you don't abide by them.

And while you are aware that this attention to detail is certainly what Britten wanted, at no time does Steuart pull out the 'because Ben told me' card. And he absolutely never mentions that his mother was in the original cast of *The Beggar's Opera* or that it was the first opera he conducted for the English Opera Group. It is arguably this reluctance to blow his own trumpet, to brag about his pedigree, that has kept Steuart out of the various musical directorships and conducting posts for which he is eminently qualified.

I've never heard the piece before and I'm struck by Britten's lightness of touch; the modern, characteristic arrangements never overwhelm the tunes, but give them a zestiness. Britten had that rare ability to blur the lines between classicism and modernity, to weave traditional material into a more radical cloth, and leave the listener wondering whether something that sounded familiar was entirely new or old and borrowed.

The recording sessions are relaxed and fun, a novel experience for me. The only tension arises because the cast has brought an array of character accents for the dialogue scenes, and Michael Geliot, who is directing these scenes, thinks we should speak the lines in the clipped tones of the post-war British middle-class. It's a drawing-room comedy, he argues, not a gritty East End drama. We compromise, though Steuart stays out of the discussion and focuses on the music. What he doesn't like are 'funny accents' while we sing. He's having none of that.

The concert is widely praised, and so is the recording when it is released the following year. Yet the piece remains rarely played and its conductor underappreciated.

FOUR

So be it

In his biography of Britten, Humphrey Carpenter writes:

> Anne Wood recalls the crisis over Lesley Bedford, who sang Lucia in the first production of *The Rape of Lucretia* and Emmie in the original *Albert Herring,* both juvenile roles, though she was approaching middle age. 'It was grotesque. And it suddenly came to the point when Ben saw that it was grotesque. And he could not, he *could not* make up his mind to say anything to her. I had to do it. And she was distraught.' Steuart Bedford says his mother had fallen entirely under Britten's spell, and agrees she was utterly crushed by the rejection.

I don't think she did overstep the mark, become too friendly. Humphrey Carpenter got his information from me. But Britten didn't close up on her. Yes, he got Anne Wood to tell her and of course she was very sad about it, but she didn't complain to Ben, and that's what was crucial to their relationship.

Just before Lesley went into hospital for the operation on her neck, Pears departed to New York for a few weeks, leaving Britten in Aldeburgh to compose. Lesley was with Britten when he went. In his first letter to Pears in New York, Britten wrote:

> I loathed, more than any moment of my silly life, leaving you. Thank God I was with Lesley, because I made a fool of myself in the car.

Originally Britten and Pears had planned to undertake a concert tour in the autumn of 1948, arranged by Ralph Hawkes, who was based at the Boosey & Hawkes office in New York. But Britten had to cancel the tour because of ill health, and as Pears unexpectedly found himself free for quite a long period, he decided to go to the States regardless and take the opportunity to study with the singing teacher Clytie Mundy. It's possible that he simply needed a break from the intensity of the relationship with Britten, as well as the opportunity to exercise his more active libido. The cancelled tour was rescheduled for 1949.

Britten's health suffered as his anxiety deepened about their relationship. By the end of 1948 he was being X-rayed for stomach ulcers, but none were found.

After Lesley's operation, Britten, who was now working on *Spring Symphony*, wrote to her from Aldeburgh:

I am so glad to have had a wire from Leslie that op's successfully over & no complications. Now I suppose you've got to lie terribly still & you'll get *very* impatient, I'm sure! I'll look out some books for you now – but I'm afraid my library is a bit one-eyed at the moment, either E. M. Forster or Arthur Ransome, & you'll know the first by heart, & the second will be *much* too exciting! However I'll try & find something nice for you. A nice soporific.

My work is going slowly, but more nicely now. Poor Peter isn't enjoying his New York over-much – a bit lonely, I think. But he's working well & long – so that will cheer him up.

I hope you have good news from the kids. I've just had a wild letter from Humphrey [Maud] – 'his classics beak is a stinking good man', so *that's* alright! Mind you come to Aldeburgh, the moment you're let out. Couldn't Leslie drive you down, & we could then talk boats. Cherubs are the thing, I believe!

Britten wrote to Pears in New York:

Lesley has had her op. Successfully & without complications. Send her a p.c. if you've time – to the Westminster hospital. There is a large photostat of a J. C. Bach aria from Brit. Mus. – d'you want it sent?

A few days later he wrote, from Aldeburgh, to Pears again:

I had a long talk with Lesley on the phone today – she is out of hospital, & at home with Leslie & all the boys around her! Scarcely peaceful – but she seems fine. As soon as she is ready to travel Leslie will drive her down here for some days to recuperate. Morgan [E. M. Forster] may come next week too, which will be nice.

Lesley also wrote to Pears in New York and on 2 November he wrote back:

Thank you so much for your letter – I was very glad to have it – & so sorry you were feeling as though you'd been pick-axed in the throat. It's a very vulnerable part of one's body and I know after tonsils I felt just the same – though one rather soon got over it. Hope you're feeling better now. I know those radios in hospital wards – when I came from 'under' my tonsils, the first noise I heard was the fall of France over the radio, & I felt like going back 'under' again! People have no ears! It's the same here – Meg Mundy, the daughter of Mrs M., did her first play broadcast last night – it was unbelievably awful (she was very good), a whole play squeezed into 20 minutes, with 10 minutes advertising U.S. steel at the end! What a place this is! Too awful most of the time, but some very sweet people. I'm enjoying my lessons with Clytie enormously – the noise I make now on a top C! I work every day with her & practise in her house and I do think she's incredibly good.

One should feel a sort of triangle inside one's face – very wide inside at the top, and high high cheekbones! Tongue can be up if it wants to, but tip should touch bottom of front teeth nearly all the time! And smile! Oh dear how one must smile!

Tomorrow I'm going to learn how to sing [Lehár's] 'Dein ist mein [ganzes] Herz' like Tauber – as I'm getting rather fat from American food you won't recognise me to look at or to listen to!

I'm longing to be back in good old dreary old England!

In mid-November, Lesley took up Britten's invitation to convalesce at Crag House for a week, which coincided with Pears's return from America. There was another row between Britten and Pears.

Thank you [...] for your sweet note about the week you spent with us here. I am so very glad it helped to get you better, because it also gave me a great deal of pleasure to have you here! I am sorry you got muddled a bit in a purely domestic tiff (I gather over the weekend too – in telephone calls!) – it was really all my fault for being touchy and silly – caused largely by my tummy & general pregnancy (the first, happily cured, the second – even worse to date!) I do hope it didn't leave a nasty taste in your mouth – but I don't think it can have done, because I know you're too large-hearted to worry about that kind of silliness.

Peter sends love – he is much less tired now, & we are working hard together, he singing like a civilised Siegfried – a tremendous din!!!

Britten passed on some advice from his GP brother-in-law, Kit Welford, who was married to Britten's sister Beth:

Don't try singing too soon, please, even if it means missing a date or two. I am sure (so is Kit) that there is nothing fundamentally changed, but you *might* do harm by rushing it. Rest is jolly good sometimes!

With Lesley convalescing, Britten and Pears headed to Europe for a concert tour. Afterwards, back in Aldeburgh, Britten wrote to Lesley:

I am so sorry not to have written before, but as you might imagine Holland was a tremendous rush, & since I got back life has been very complicated. The trouble is that my tummy went *all* wrong again – even on the journey over! I had to cancel one concert, & only staggered through the others – Poor Peter, singing beautifully all the time, had a very worrying time.

Anyhow, here I am, back in Aldeburgh in bed – & the Doctor warns me that it may be *three* months of just lying around this time. I am X-rayed tomorrow so I shall soon know the worst – but I believe that even if it isn't serious, the rest will be enforced.

What a bore! At least I can go on writing, but all our concerts & tours abroad to go . . . I could kick myself! *And* I shan't see your kids in the holidays, nor nothing!

Please tell Leslie that I don't know *when* I shall be able to go over & see about that boat – hope there's no hurry! Is he well? Give him lots of love from me – & the kids when they get home. I hope you have a rip-roaring Christmas.

Thank you so much for being so nice to me before I went off – I loved being with you.

I hope the neck is absolutely well now – how goes the singing?

I hope you didn't go to Aberdeen, & enjoyed Dave's performance – & Stewy's!

And after Christmas, for which Steuart – now nine – had given Britten a tie, he wrote again to the Bedfords:

Thank you for sending the Scottish songs (can't *promise* anything, but you never can tell). Thank you more than I can say for the Bach records, thank you for the Ransome (most welcome & I'm now *complete*!), thank you for the sweet letters, (most charming and helpful) etc etc etc . . .

Please give the two little ones the enclosed notes, sorry they aren't longer or bigger but I'm not good at letters nowadays. I'm cutting away, owing to one thing or another, for a few days now [. . .] Hope life will be smoother when I get back. I will let you know how the future plans itself & whether I'm allowed up to town, if not . . . perhaps you could come down – wouldn't it be fun?

And to Steuart – now nine – Britten wrote:

I think it is very clever of you to choose me such a beautiful tie. I have lots of ties (at a guess about twenty-five), but I like this one the best, & wear it most often!

I am glad that you had a lovely Christmas, but I wish I had been able to spend some of it with you.

We had some very rough seas, and alot of the beach has got washed away. Unless they put breakwaters or a big wall in front of us, it looks as if we might be washed away too. Perhaps I ought to sleep in a rubber boat in future.

Yoxford, March 2018

Steuart and I are having a few days together, working on the book. The plan is simple: I'll point a video camera at him, ask him a lot of questions, and we'll have a recording from which I can reconstruct his life. There are also other sources – articles and interviews – which I can use, which were collected long before Parkinson's reared its ugly head. Some of these he has in his study, and some are in the Britten–Pears Archive.

The filming is a mixed success. Steuart will be doing fine, with excellent recollection, and then suddenly he hits a wall. 'Damn. I suddenly have no idea what the word is that I want. That's the disease, I'm afraid. It's there in front of me, but I can't find it.'

His rainbow array of pills makes his throat dry and hoarse, and sometimes I struggle to hear him. Too often, when he is struggling to home in on a thought, I jump in and offer suggestions, but this only adds to the confusion. Sometimes the silence is agonising. Sometimes Steuart, in his struggle to find the right word, simply goes for it, and a seemingly bizarre word is offered in its place. In one of these conversations he says 'pizzicato' when I think he means to say 'person'.

On another occasion, weary from a disturbed night – nights are when he can become fretful and confused – he falls asleep in mid-sentence, the camera still rolling.

We visit the Britten–Pears Archive together. It's an extraordinary collection, housed in an elegant building beside the Red House, where Britten and Pears lived for many years. I drive Steuart there.

'Don't park in the main car park. Let's park in front of the house on the left, before we get to the main house. That's where I always used to park.'

So we do. A brick path takes a slightly longer route around a shrubby bed up to the entrance of the Archive.

'Oh bugger that. I'm not going all that way round.' And he cuts straight through the shrubs with me in his wake.

He tells me he came to the Red House even before it belonged to Britten and Pears, when the house was owned by the artist Mary Potter and her husband, the writer Stephen Potter.

'We met the Potters on the beach and they invited us up for tea.'

The senior archivists treat Steuart like royalty, which is pleasing. We are shown to the reading room by an intern, who tells us that another reader will also be using the archive that day, an American academic who is writing a history of the Aldeburgh Festival. When he shows up, he is 'honoured and thrilled' to meet Steuart, and Steuart responds with his customary self-deprecating modesty, while quite enjoying the flattery. The academic disappears behind his laptop and we attack the several boxes of old programmes that the archivists have dug out for us.

We converse in library whispers, but it isn't long before Steuart has said something that makes me laugh, or I have said something rude back to him, and we are chuckling wheezily and noisily. The intern rises from her desk.

'Can I remind you, please, that you are not alone, and that we have another reader. Please keep your conversation down!'

We make faces at each other, like scolded schoolchildren, and return to our work.

That evening we meet Oliver Knussen for a curry. Steuart and Olly were once joint Artistic Directors of the Aldeburgh Festival, but they rarely see each other and never socialise. There's a wariness between them that is difficult to fathom, a not quite forgotten or forgiven disagreement from the past. Or maybe it is a good old-fashioned professional rivalry. Somehow, the Venn diagram of their personalities doesn't overlap as much as I had hoped, except in the shyness department. But the evening is jolly enough and they share stories of the old days, happiest when finding a common enemy to complain about. Chief among these are one particularly difficult Festival co-director, and Donald Mitchell – Britten's publisher, one of his executors and a trustee of the Britten–Pears Foundation – who was inclined to make unilateral planning decisions for the Festival, even though the Festival wasn't his turf. (Mitchell also committed the cardinal sin of calling Steuart 'Stewy', frequently and in public.) As it turns out, this curry will be the last time Steuart and Olly ever meet. Exactly four months later, just days after his sixty-sixth birthday, Olly dies.

From a drawer in his study Steuart pulls out a large old manilla envelope, overstuffed with papers.

'You'll enjoy this lot,' he says. I pull out the papers. They are dozens of letters, most still in their original envelopes, and postcards, all from Britten and Pears, to Steuart, his mother, and his various siblings.

A postcard to Steuart has an additional 'STEWY' scrawled in pencil on it.

'David must have done that.'

FIVE

What lies in wait for me here?

BETWEEN 1948 AND 1953, after my parents had bought the cottage opposite the Golden Key in Snape, we saw quite a lot of Ben and Peter. We would load up my father's soft-top Rover with piles of suitcases and all kinds of stuff and head up to Suffolk for our summer holidays. The cottage – actually two cottages joined together – was very basic. There was no electricity, no loo – just an Elsan in a hut in the garden, which my father used to empty every so often. We'd cycle everywhere and go sailing. My father kept a boat at Orford, but I didn't like sailing very much.

There'd be lots of games of ping-pong at Crag House and Ben always played to win. He was childish in childish company, but he didn't like to lose at games.

We used to have these trips out in Ben's old Rolls-Royce. We'd drive off to Waxham or somewhere and spend the day by the sea, and then come back for tea. Cake, egg sandwiches, that sort of thing – but not cheese for me. For some reason I didn't like cheese.

There'd be a great gang of us; the three of us boys and Sebastian Welford, the son of Ben's sister Beth. Sometimes the rest of the Welford family as well – as many as would fit in that old Rolls. Ben and Peter would do anything to amuse us.

We started a very, very childish and naughty game in the car. The road into Aldeburgh passes the golf course, and the first or second tee is right by the road. I think my father started it off, naughtily and irresponsibly hooting the horn just as someone had raised their club, thereby making the golfer miss his shot or putting him off his stroke. Ben thought this was a wonderful idea. One day, Peter was driving the Rolls – the horn on the Rolls made a noise like nothing on earth, a dreadful, screeching honk – and when we got to the golf course, Peter put his hand on the horn and kept it down all the way along for about half a mile, shattering the peace of the neighbourhood.

In those days, Snape Bridge was small, narrow and humpbacked. They eventually replaced it and all the old bricks ended up in the garden walls of the Red House. But back then most people would slow down and approach it rather gingerly. Not Ben. There was no question of him waiting for anyone coming the other way. He'd accelerate as he came towards it and take it at high speed, and the whole car would take off.

◊

In February of 1949, Britten and Pears took a holiday in Venice. Peter sent a postcard to Lesley:

The beauty of this place is past description & though it has now got cold & the wind blows, it has been a wonderful 10 days – a very nice hotel with rooms looking over the lagoon & the Doge's Palace, wonderful pictures, the sun shining all the time, coffee by St Mark's in the open, excursions by land & sea, church after church, and all without traffic – not a car – not a horse – not a sound – heavenly. Tomorrow (Friday) night we go to Rapello for a week – back on Sat 12th.

Little could they have imagined at the time that twenty-four years later, Lesley's youngest son, little Stewy, would be conducting the world premiere of Britten's final opera, *Death in Venice*, nor indeed that, during a run of performances of the opera at La Fenice opera house, Steuart and Pears would also drink coffee by St Mark's.

On his return, Britten wrote to Lesley from Crag House. Lesley had clearly shared some concerns about Steuart's brother, David. Over the next few years, she would often ask Britten for advice and he seemed to relish the opportunity to provide it.

> I have been thinking & feeling a lot with you [. . .] exactly *how* is difficult to write in a letter. Actually the most important thing is that Leslie & David get on so well, & David will need him more & more as time goes on. That is the thing to be aimed at – & how it is to be achieved I know will gradually become clear to you. I fancy you know already. If I can help in any way – even just by being an old bit of blotting paper – write and say how.

In June, some of the Bedfords went to hear Pears sing in Southwark Cathedral. The following day Peter wrote to Lesley:

> I think I saw signs of assorted Bedfords at Southwark last night – but what with hay-fever, sparrows, London South Eastern & Chatham Railway and the ignorance of acoustics of Gothic master-masons, not to mention the sweet shyness of Rural Music School Choirs, you cannot have enjoyed it very much! But bless you for coming –

Although it was his brother David who was setting his heart on becoming a composer, Steuart too was working on his harmony and counterpoint. In August 1949 he sent Britten a chorale. Britten responded:

> Thank you for sending me the chorale. I like it. Is the new piece (the one from *these* holidays) better still? I miss you all here – but I'm going away to-morrow too – Boo-hoo.

This spurred on Steuart to pen a fantasia.

Dear Stewy,
   Thank you for sending
me the chorale. I like
it. Is the new piece
(the one from their
holidays) better still?
I miss you all here –
but I'm going away to-morrow
to – Boo-hoo. Luv Ben.

Stewart Bedford S,
16 Heathgate
Golders Green
London N.W. 11

Postcard from Benjamin Britten to Steuart Bedford, September 1949.

Britten and Pears toured Europe and the United States, with Leslie Bedford meeting up with them in New York. Lesley wrote to them both with some help from David and Steuart. Peter wrote to her from Los Angeles at the end of November 1949:

Your letters have been manna in the desert & as welcome as they possibly could be. Thank you so very much. Needless to say, there is only *one* thing we are longing for at the moment – to be back in England & with you all again.

It was lovely having Leslie with us – really a breath of fresh air amid all the noise & fuss & tension & horror of New York. How we loathed it! & what a relief it was to get to the sweet unsophisticated Middle West colleges – Canada was lovely too though madly rushed – & now this absurd but rather sweet place!

Ben very much appreciated a twin communication from Dave & Stewie – Keeping him abreast of the football news & the movie situation at Redhill! I'm very glad Dave's knee is better, & Stewie's Fantasia sounds very impressive – I can see his concentrated frown at the keyboard. How was the Bach? & which was it, I wonder? Oh to be in England!

They have produced what they call a smog here (smoke & fog) which they think is terrible but it just seems a heat haze to me. [Carl] Ebert is busy producing Albert [*Albert Herring*] (!) at the University here & we may go to a rehearsal (God help us!). We have three concerts here with the L.A. Phil, Ben conducting Purcell St Cecilia's Ode Overture – Orpheus Brit [a suite of songs orchestrated by Britten from Purcell's *Orpheus Britannicus* collections] – Britten – Grimes Interludes; Serenade; Young Person's Guide. Lovely program, very nicely played, fairly well sung!, characteristically conducted! America makes me so nervous that I have hardly been able to make a sound with nerves, but it's getting better now.

Britten wrote shortly after his thirty-sixth birthday:

No time for more than a note – Peter's told you our news & how we long to be back – & will be soon! We count the days like at prep school. Dave's & Stewy's letters are *wonderful* & help us alot – they're darlings to write so much. And you, my dearest Lesley, your letter arrived plumb *on* my birthday in Los Angeles - a miracle of timing! It is lovely that you're singing Bach on 22nd.

Our concerts here are nice – good orchestra, friendly people – different from beastly, hateful, sinister, stupid, snobbish, unimportant New York – (I don't like New York)

The first few days of 1950 saw the usual spate of Christmas thank-you letters. Lesley had sent books by the seventeenth-century poet Edmund Waller and by Helen Waddell – probably her novel *Peter Abelard*. Britten was known to be interested in the story of Abelard and Héloïse, possibly as a subject for an opera (with Ronald Duncan) or as a cantata (with Eric Crozier). As the year turned Pears was struck down with shingles during performances of

Handel's *Messiah* in the north of England – hence his allusions to the arias 'Comfort Ye' and 'Every Valley':

First of all thank you so much for the lovely presents – the Waddell moved me deeply – in fact on Christmas Day I read the bit about the Star and had a quiet cry in bed all by myself, while the others were at Church! The Waller I have not yet looked at properly.

Then it was lovely to have your letter full of family news – Peter's school, & Dave's speech and all. What a hectic time you must have had & how lovely it must have been!

I thought you might ring up & am very glad you weren't daunted by Ben's transparent Doppelgänger at the telephone! How anyone is even taken in I don't know. You must get over your telephone manners – they're terrible I know – but you are always welcome, my dear!

This shingles is a most hateful complaint. It was descending on me rapidly while I was Comforting and every valleying Bolton and Huddersfield and the night journey without sleeper afterwards didn't help – it was exceedingly painful to begin with and remains much less so for some time, but, as it is an affliction of the nervous system, apparently, one is all of a jangles for ages and feels as well as a kitten and far less playful. Being in the head too is a bore; one feels more than usually silly. However my Mr B says 'rest' – so rest I shall! Which will be lovely – nothing probably til mid-February, and a holiday in Switzerland before that, I hope. I think this attack may easily clean up the whole of my annoying Head Situation!

I wish I was going to be able to come and see you all before all the decorations get taken down & the Christmas spirit starts to evaporate, or do you keep them up all the holidays? I want to hear Stew play his Fantasia too.

Today is lovely down here – mild and calm, with the gulls sitting on the water, watching the anglers compete. It's a relief after two days of high seas and East Winds –

Dear Lesley, much love to you and to Leslie and the boys. Have a lovely holiday all together. I hope Dave has fun at his cricket school. (Perhaps 'fun''s not the right word!)

Britten's thank-you note to Lesley reported on the invalid: 'Peter is slowly getting better but it's a hellish complaint.' By the same post he wrote to David Bedford:

At last a letter from me! So *very* sorry I haven't written you a letter before to thank you for the lovely scarf, but I have been so terribly, terribly busy that letter-writing was quite out of the question.

I love the scarf and wear it always. It is a lovely colour, and keeps me beautifully warm, even in the cold east winds which blow along the beach here. Thank you very much. Peter loved your letter, & thanks you very much for it. He is feeling a little better, & hopes to be well enough to go to Switzerland for some sun & mountains which should make him quite well again. I shall probably take him to London on Tuesday – will you be there or back at school? I'd love to see you, & play you at ping-pong, although I expect you've been practising so hard that you'd beat me easily! I've been playing squash once or twice; do you play that? It's a lovely game – *very* fast. I think you'd be awfully good at it. How go the cricket coachings?

The sea defences are progressing very well – but very noisily, just outside our house. The pile-driver works all day, & so do the concrete mixers, and a giant scooper which takes up great buckets of shingle and waves them around in the air (often over our garden) before plonking them down somewhere else.

Here are a few stamps – not many but I'll try & save some more.

Please give my love to Stewy & and the enclosed note to Peter.

By February, Pears was feeling much better. Meanwhile, Peter Bedford, who had turned eighteen in December, had been called up for National Service. Pears wrote to Lesley from Scotland:

Here we are almost as far North as we shall venture – only 15 miles South of Aberdeen, but I suppose that simply isn't Scotland for you yet – we're among the Sassenachs still! Anyway it's extremely beautiful, and we adore it – we've been very lucky with the weather – two absolutely perfect early spring days – bright seas and wonderful skies. Yesterday we went for a long walk along the cliffs here, past ruined castles and such – Dare we say it? We prefer the East Coast to the West, at least such as we have seen. [...]

We're having a wee bittie party after Spring Symphony on March 9th at Melbury Rd. Do come & bring as many of your contingent as may be coming – (tho' I bet you won't!)

The party was to celebrate the first UK performance of *Spring Symphony* at the Royal Albert Hall. A week later Britten acknowledged a letter from Lesley about the work with a postcard from Aldeburgh:

You shouldn't have troubled to write – but I'm glad you did. It was very sweet and remarkably sane for 2 a.m.! So glad you're seeing Peter P. tonight. How's the other Peter getting on? Thanks for the children's letters – much appreciated. I've written to them – dreadful how one writes *that* kind of letter and neglects the business ones!

Meanwhile, the ten year-old Steuart was progressing well in his music studies at Hillsbrow prep school:

My parents would come and visit me occasionally on Saturday afternoons, as was allowed at boarding school in those days. One Saturday my mother drove down in her car, the Little Biscuit, with Ben and a much older man whom I didn't know, and whom Ben introduced as 'Morgan'. This turned out to be E. M. Forster, but at the time I had absolutely no idea who that was. Morgan insisted that I play the piano to him, so my mother and Ben went off for a stroll and I led Morgan off to the school music room, which was basically a dingy old shed with an absolutely frightful piano. Ghastly. But we went in there and he sat down and I played him some Mozart.

Then Ben and my mother turned up and Ben played the Mozart G major Sonata (K283) on this terrible old upright piano, and of course when I heard Ben play it, I immediately had to learn it too. It was quite a hypnotic fascination. I wouldn't dream of playing the piano in front of Ben though. He was the Grand Master as far as I was concerned and I was far too nervous.

Ben would play anything that was sitting on the piano. He came to our house once with his arm in a sling. It must have been in 1953 when he had bursitis. The Fourth Beethoven Concerto was on the piano and he whizzed through the tricky bits with just his left hand.

E. M. Forster spent much of the summer of 1950 at Crag House, working with Britten and Eric Crozier on *Billy Budd*. Michael Tippett, who was recuperating from hepatitis, was also a visitor that summer. David Bedford remembers 'a bumper-car battle' during the Aldeburgh Carnival 'between myself, Ben and Michael Tippett which caused total chaos with all of us wearing ludicrous silly hats'. (He dates the memory to 1953, but 1950 seems the likelier date.) Steuart, meanwhile, stayed behind in Snape, 'copying out a Bach fugue'.

In the autumn of 1950 David Bedford moved on to public school. His father, Leslie, and older brother Peter had both gone to Marlborough College, but with Britten's and Pears's encouragement, David was sent instead to Pears's old alma mater, Lancing College. One of the masters' wives at Lancing, Esther Neville-Smith, had taken a maternal interest in Pears and Britten, and they too were devoted to her and would visit her often. It was Esther who in 1947 offered £100 to commission *Saint Nicolas* for the school's centenary, a work that Pears would return regularly to his old school to perform.

With his brothers Peter in the army and David at Lancing, Steuart was now alone at his prep school, where he excelled not only at the piano but on the cricket pitch.

Britten and Pears, holidaying in Sicily, sent Lesley a postcard.

Having the loveliest, v certainly hottest holiday ever! Blue sea, sweet Italian town, wonderful Greek temple, and lots of heavenly sun. We're both as brown as berries. I do hope all goes well with you – love to Leslie, Dave & Stewy & Peter when you write.

Ben

There's an old man who carries a can of water down twisty roads to water some minute trees that are baby olives, I suppose, just below our hotel, on the side of the mountains, & as he goes back and forth he sings a weird primitive folk ditty at the top of his voice. It sounds like darkest Africa, but it's all part of this incredible place.

Much love to you all,

Peter

On 14 November, Lesley sang with Pears again, in a concert at the Friends' House, Euston Road, promoted by the English Opera Group. She sang Clorinda to Pears's Testo in Monteverdi's *Il combattimento di Tancredi e Clorinda*. Maurice Bevan was the Tancredi. Britten was in the audience.

Britten's birthday came around again, and shortly afterwards, Christmas, and in the new year, another bout of ping-pong at the Bedfords'. Lesley had sent Britten a book by Goldsworthy Lowes Dickinson, the political scientist and philosopher, a pacifist and instrumental in the formation of the League of Nations. He was a friend and colleague of E. M. Forster at Cambridge University. He had died in 1932.

Sweet of you to send me the Lowes Dickinson. I had been re-reading E.M.F.'s book on him recently, & this comes most opportunely, & I look forward to reading it alot. He was a great man.

I had a quiet birthday – work in the morning, & the afternoon I took Beth & her children out to Shingle Street for tea – gay & wild.

Peter is down here, singing Nicolas at Ipswich & Bury, so we are belatedly celebrating the great day!

I had sweet letters from Dave & Stewy. I am glad they seem well & cheerful. I hear great things via Peter of Dave's scholarship papers. When is the exam?

I did so admire you in the Monteverdi. Your performance was just right for the wonderful work it is. I hope you were pleased too.

Britten spent that Christmas with George and Marion Harewood and their baby son, David. It was from Harewood House that he wrote his thank-you letters:

Thank you ever so for the lovely books – you always choose so sympathetically & cleverly, & I always find lots to like or to provoke in what you send me! I loved the boys' tie – brilliant even for them! Please tell them that I am writing. When I get back from here, &, most important, that I'm going to desert Billy Budd in the middle of Jan (17th–19th) & come up to London. I hereby challenge them to epic matches of ping-pong.

I am sure you had the most 'smashing' or whatever the latest adjective is, Christmas. I hope you're not too worn out! Did Peter manage to get back, for a day or two at least?

My god-child is very sweet and was Christened in great style. Marion is adorable with him – an excellent mother.

This was the year of *Billy Budd*, and Britten was hard at work throughout 1951 preparing the opera for its December premiere.

In the autumn, Peter Bedford was demobbed from the army and went up to his father's alma mater, King's College, Cambridge, to read classics. Although he didn't sing in the famous chapel choir, Peter was a fine baritone, nurturing ambitions to become a professional singer like his mother and grandmother.

My mother used to take us up to King's to visit Peter, and we'd have tea in his rooms and then go to Evensong. By now my piano playing was pretty good – I was playing Mozart concertos by the time I left Hillsbrow – but when I heard the organ in King's chapel, I decided what I wanted to do. I wanted to take up the organ and become the organ scholar at King's College, Cambridge. So, that was it, I had a plan.

The flaw in the plan was a lack of an organ at Hillsbrow on which to learn:

During the Snape holidays we would drive around, asking the vicars of local churches if I could have an afternoon playing the organ. Only a couple said yes.

In the midst of rehearsals for *Billy Budd* at the Royal Opera House, Pears went down to Lancing and reported back to Lesley, while also inviting her to a dress rehearsal of *Billy Budd*:

> Thank you so very much for your sweet letter of too long ago – I believe I am seeing a little light at last about the voice! 'Light! Yes though it blind mine eyes – '!
> I was down at Lancing for 18 hours yesterday. Dave came with some chaps and had tea. He seemed entirely happy & radiant – it was very good to see him – you needn't worry about him there!

After *Billy Budd* had opened at Covent Garden on 1 December, Lesley wrote to Britten, and he dutifully replied on a postcard:

Your letter gave me great pleasure – thank you so much for writing about B Budd. Also very glad to hear how successful Lancing is being – that's great news.

Correspondence had become faltering and a little awkward. But after Lesley had written more 'fan mail', this time about his new *Canticle II: 'Abraham and Isaac'*, which she had heard on the radio, Britten again wrote back:

Your letter about Abraham & Isaac gave me great pleasure. You are sweet to have written, & you need never worry that I shall be bored to hear from you! I love your warm praise – for seriously, if you & your friends are pleased with my music, that's what I write it for. I'm naturally glad that you like my youngest child, because, as is so often the case – he gave me great trouble in coming into the world!

I hope you have good news of all your dear ones. I hope to be able to drive down to Lancing with Peter later this term, so I hope to see Dave in all his glory!

In March, Britten and Pears took a skiing holiday in Austria with the Harewoods, the dedicatees of *Billy Budd*. It was during this holiday that Britten started to divert his attention from writing a children's opera, *Tyco the Vegan*, to a commission from Covent Garden, engineered largely by George Harewood: *Gloriana*. Pears and Britten wrote Lesley a postcard:

[Pears:] The mountains are behaving themselves quite wonderfully. Snow at night, sun in the day & we have just made a day trek up & ski-ing down – our ski-ing is not yet too marvellous but it doesn't matter –

[Britten:] Most exhausting & exhilarating holiday imaginable!

Now twelve and into his final term at prep school, Steuart became captain of the cricket second eleven: 'I was quite good in the slips.' But while he was entirely capable of playing Mozart's concertos, there was, alas, no school orchestra to accompany him.

In May, David Bedford heard the *Spring Symphony* and wrote to Britten about it. Britten's reply included encouragement for a proposed performance of the *Five Flower Songs* he had composed in 1950 for unaccompanied chorus:

Thank you so much for your nice letter. I am so glad you listened to the Spring Symphony and enjoyed it. I couldn't be at the hall because I was away in Paris (conducting Billy Budd with Peter) but I heard the second broadcast all right. I was also glad that you're working so hard at the Flower Songs – I'll try to get down to the concert but I can't promise at the moment, because I've got so many things to do. I'd also like to see you play cricket. How's that going this term? Are you beautifully on form? I expect you find the standard a bit higher than in Redhill don't you?

It's been horribly wet here for most of Whitsun – but today it's lovely in Paris. I'm writing this in the garden before breakfast, and the fishermen are going by outside the gate with fish they've been catching.

Throughout most of the Bedfords' summer holidays that year Britten and Pears were on a motoring tour of France and Italy, again with the Harewoods, again discussing *Gloriana*, and giving the odd recital too. From Menton, on the Côte d'Azur, they sent the Bedfords a postcard:

[Pears:] How are you all? We are having a very hot drive back into Italy (Venice) but the sea is wonderful here & it is covered at the moment with sailing boats competing in the Regatta – back on August 24th or so –

[Britten:] This sea feels *quite* different from the Aldeburgh one – almost boiling – but all the same we long for Suffolk!

When they got back in late August, interrupted only by the Thorpeness cricket match in early September in which David's (and thereby Steuart's) vocabulary was expanded by a furious Lord Harewood, Britten set to work on composing *Gloriana*. Pears set off on a recital tour, but this time without Britten at the piano.

Steuart, who had just turned thirteen, suddenly fell seriously ill. It was an illness that would affect the rest of his life.

Lyon, France, 1994

Steuart and I are puffing and panting our way up the long flights of steps to the Basilica that sits at the top of the steep hill to the west of the city, above the old town. We have just had a good lunch at which Steuart ordered the *quenelles de brochet*. Steuart, given the choice, always orders the *quenelles de brochet*.

In 1991, the Festival d'Aix-en-Provence presented a new production of *A Midsummer Night's Dream*, conducted by Steuart and directed by Robert Carsen. It was a huge success, so much so that the Festival revived it the very next year and then organised a tour throughout France in 1994. (The production has subsequently gone to London, Barcelona, Milan, Beijing and Philadelphia. While the production and its design were the obvious stand-outs, the less-lauded factor in its success was the quality of the music-making. It would become clear in the years ahead that, without the right conductor in the pit, the production lost a good deal of its allure.)

And so, here we are, after a sell-out run of performances at the Opéra-Comique in Paris, on the second leg of the tour. As we heave ourselves up the steep incline we talk about philosophy, as you are wont to do after a good plate of *quenelles*.

I first met Steuart eleven years earlier but I haven't spent any time with him until this production of the *Dream*. I found him a bit terrifying at first, distant. Lodged somewhere in my mind was a memory that someone had described him as somebody with a volcanic temper. I don't know who told me this, and I have never witnessed it – tetchy, yes; volcanic, no – but I was wary in case of a possible eruption. An eruption never happened. Perhaps my source, or my memory, was wrong. I also felt that we *should* get on, given I have close friends who like Steuart so it made sense that I should like him too.

It has taken me the last three years to realise that it isn't that Steuart is unfriendly, it's that he is deeply shy, and the way he connects most happily with people is in the exchange of mock-grumpy banter. This suits me very well. It's right up my alley. If Steuart is rude to you, it almost certainly means he likes you and feels relaxed with you. So we sat at lunch, piling pike-mousse dumplings swimming in cream into our faces and exchanging insults, and this is how our relationship will continue up the hillside and pretty much for decades to come.

Steuart is someone who doesn't mind being on his own, which is useful for a conductor or an itinerant soloist. It's a trait that can pass for anti-social, but it's really not.

As we climb the hill we talk about a topic that's never far from the freelance musician's mind when he's away from home: What's It All About?

I'm a relative novice at this, the juggling of a career and home life. Steuart has been doing it for a while longer. Our children are much the same age, so despite our age difference of nineteen years we have that in common.

'You know those people you see at airports? Those men you see rushing to get to the gate, fretting at security, complaining that the queue isn't going fast enough and they have a plane to catch? Well, I'm trying to rule that out of my life. I'm determined not to be one of those men, and I suppose you could say I'm working on myself about that,' says Steuart. (Aha, good tip, as I realise he is actually passing on advice to me.)

We discuss the book *Zen and the Art of Motorcycle Maintenance*, which anyone at the time with an eye to understanding the human condition has on their bookshelf.

Somewhere near the top of the hill, the Basilica before us, he says, 'I've been struggling to understand the difference between inductive and deductive logic, and I'm sure that the way it's explained in that bloody motorcycle book is the wrong way round. I'm sure he's got it completely wrong!'

I honestly can't remember how it's explained but I promise to have a look when I'm home after the Lyon dates.

Back at home a week or so later I look up the passage on logic, and when I think I've figured it out, I compose a waggish one-page parable of my own based on two travelling salesmen in the Wild West, Indy Uctivelogic and his brother Deed, who keep having their boots stolen. Pleased with myself, I fax it to Steuart. Not long afterwards the phone rings.

'Have you gone completely fucking mad? What a load of utter nonsense.'

'Well, yes, obviously it's nonsense, but I think I've got it the right way round.'

'Hmmm, no, I'm not so sure about that.' Which is Steuart's way of saying *no, you're completely wrong.* It's much the same way he will haul you up for singing a wrong note: 'Yes, that B flat at the beginning of the bar . . . I'm not totally convinced you're singing the right note.' Or, if you're singing too loud, 'Do you really have to make that awful racket? It's not *Tosca*, you know.'

Or the way he'll warn you that a role you've just accepted might be trickier than you had imagined: 'Oh God, you'll never get that right.'

SIX

My head is heavy, my eyelids ache

Towards the end of his holidays in Snape, just a few days after the Thorpeness cricket match he now remembers so vividly, Steuart was struck down by a very high fever, abdominal pain and chronic diarrhoea. A doctor was called, then an ambulance, and Steuart was whisked off at high speed to Hendon Isolation Hospital in north London, over a hundred miles away. The initial verdict was that Steuart had contracted dysentery, but eventually the Harley Street gastroenterologist (and editor of the medical journal *Gut*) Francis Avery Jones gave a diagnosis of salmonella typhinurium.

I was put in a ward with some old men and a smaller child. There was a nurse whom I remember as being quite hideously cruel. I wasn't allowed any visitors and I was forced to drink vast quantities – it seemed like a gallon a day – of some disgusting, green medicine called 'Hartley's Liquid'. Eventually, after two weeks, my parents kicked up a major fuss and almost removed me by force. I think there may even have been an enquiry; I don't know what happened. I was taken home to Hampstead Garden Suburb and lived, quarantined in my bedroom, where our GP came every day to give me cortisone injections.

In Aldeburgh, still remembering the cricket match, Britten was kept abreast of Steuart's illness and treatment, although the full severity of his condition wasn't yet clear.

I do hope that works, & that finally after all this time dear Stewy will be returned to complete health, for him, for you, & for all of the family. It has been a most beastly time, & I hope the end is now in sight. It was lovely to catch a glimpse of them all a week or so ago. It was a curious, if amusing, occasion [. . .]

Maybe I will catch a glimpse of you the next two weeks in London? I do hope so.

It was a while before Steuart was well enough to start his first term as a music scholar at Lancing, joining the school several weeks late. His abiding memory of his first days is seeing sugar in paper packets for the first time, after rationing had been lifted.

The illness would recur regularly in the years ahead, often causing long periods of quarantine. Britten, for whom illness was a regular, debilitating burden, must surely have felt a particular empathy for his fellow sufferer, whom he also considered a young friend.

On 22 November it was Britten's birthday again, and Steuart, who was still more fascinated by Britten's abilities as a pianist than as a composer, sent him a Mozart concerto as a gift.

For some reason in those days the concertos were a bit difficult to get hold of, and he didn't have all the copies of the old Mozart Gesellschaft at the time. He often said to me, 'I wish I could get hold of K456', which is a B flat one. I used to shop around for these things in London and I suddenly came across a reprint of the miniature score. So I sent him one for his birthday, and he was over the moon about it. He played it in the next Aldeburgh Festival. It's delightful – the wonderful slow movement with variations.

Two days after his birthday, while working on *Gloriana*, Britten wrote to Lesley:

Dearest Stewy sent me a Mozart Concerto I hadn't got – such a remarkable boy to remember that! I was deeply touched, and more than ever bored that I can't get down to Lancing to see the chaps. Poor Sebastian [Britten's nephew, his sister Beth's son] crashed in his Common Entrance, rather as we'd feared, but luckily he's got a second try. I'm sure it's the school for him and we're praying that next time will be lucky!

The old Opera goes along – quite well I hope, but rather an anxiety with the time pressing on one so. It's a wonderful subject.

Excuse scribble my dear – but the days are short for all one's got to get in them, aren't they? Hope all is well with you. At any rate I hope I can get to London in the chaps' holidays so I can see them then. I miss them alot. Or are you coming to Snape?

And to Steuart he wrote:

I was delighted to get the Mozart Concerto. What a chap you are to remember that that was one of the few that I hadn't got! I hope *very* much that you haven't given up your only copy. I should hate to think that. But I am enjoying playing & reading it alot – it's a real beauty, especially the extraordinary slow movement, full of the most surprising things. Do you play it? I must say that I'm terribly tempted to play it in one of our Festival concerts sometime – in which case we must wangle your being there!

How are you? Do you approve of Lancing & does Lancing approve of you? I *had* hoped very much to get down & see you & a few other friends, but work on the Opera is so urgent & I can't leave. Perhaps after Christmas when the sketches will be finished & only the score to do. Do you like Edward Piper [the son of John and Myfanwy Piper]? I'll hear your news in the Christmas holidays, because at least I'll see you in London I hope.

Lots of love to you, & many thanks again. Behave yourself & I hope you don't get frozen stiff in this weather – the Downs can be almost as chilly as the East coast of Suffolk.

In the new year there was another exchange of letters. Britten was again at Harewood House.

You seem to have had a smashing Christmas. We *also* went Carol singing, & enjoyed it hugely – for the Friends of our Festival. We had crowds of people to stay, it seemed, & it was rather exhausting – but I've now come up here (Peter's on the move of course) & am giving my good Miss Hudson [the housekeeper] a bit of a rest, from me! The opera is going on well – but is rather absorbing – hence the horrid scrawl. I'll let you know if there's a chance of coming up these holidays.

In March 1953 the Bedfords were in Cambridge and went to a performance of *Saint Nicolas* in King's Chapel. East Anglia had suffered 'the Great Flood' at the end of January, with a death toll of over three hundred along the east coast and more than two thousand deaths in the Netherlands. Britten's home, Crag House, was inundated, and most of the village of Snape too.

Last night we were in Cambridge for the wonderful combination of you – King's Chapel – & an all-undergraduate performance. They did you so proudly Ben – & I am writing this to try to thank you. [. . .] What is that blazing quality that goes away with disillusion? I can't describe it but it was there last night in excelsis in King's Chapel – packed to suffocation. The spirit truly moved on the face of the waters. All our love & thoughts are with you during this year & we thought much of you during the 'troubles' – we went down to Snape & found the cottage had been an untouched island with water in both our poor neighbours.

The boys are in tremendous form. Pete was singing some of the solos in the great Greek play last week & had some amusing close dealings with the composer known to the students apparently as 'Prof Hadly' [Patrick Hadley, the Professor of Music at Cambridge]. Oh dear – why must he sing?

It took Britten a while to reply.

I ought to have written ages ago to thank you for your sweet letter, which gave me such great pleasure. I do regret having missed St Nicolas at King's, but I've been working like a *mad* thing to get Gloriana done, & now that's achieved (thank God) & Peter & I are off to Ireland today for a two weeks complete break! – Hence the lateness & brevity of this scribble.

I was glad for news of the boys, whom eventually I expect to see (the younger 2 at least) at Lancing over Easter, if my plan to go to Glyndebourne & on there materialises! It'll be lovely to see them happy in their surroundings. You know Beth's Sebastian is in to Lancing – after some vicissitudes! We are so pleased.

I hear better news of your health, dear Lesley. I am so pleased. Although we so seldom meet, you are often, all of you, in our thoughts.

Sometime after the flood, the Bedfords decided to sell their Snape cottage, believing that it, and in particular its rudimentary sanitary arrangements, had been to blame for their youngest son's dangerous illness.

In May, Britten and Pears bought a new London home in Chester Gate, next to Regent's Park. Nominally it was Pears's house, which was crucial at the time to avoid the impact of the law regarding homosexuality. During 1953 Britten was interviewed by the Metropolitan Police, Pears considered getting married to divert attention away from his sexuality, and their friend John Gielgud was arrested and fined for soliciting. Two men sharing the ownership of a house would have been unconscionable, and certainly dangerous.

Gloriana opened at Covent Garden to a cool reception on 8 June, and three days later Pears wrote to Lesley:

> I've never thanked you for your very sweet letter of blessings on this new house. It was very dear of you to write and I hope you will come & see it in its rather chaotic pic-nicky state. But there's nothing I should like better than another evening up with you & all the chaps. I do hope you are all of you happy & well. How are Dave's googlies and Steuart's arpeggios and Pete's low notes?!

With Snape now sold, the Bedfords no longer holidayed in Suffolk and the teenage Steuart's contact with Britten fell away.

Once I had gone to boarding school, to Lancing, I rather lost touch with Ben, because the Aldeburgh Festival took place in June when we were always at school. I think my mother kept in touch with him quite closely, although without telling us. Ben came to Lancing occasionally. He came for a *Saint Nicolas* performance, which Peter used to sing because it was Peter's old school. *Saint Nicolas* was officially written for Lancing, so whenever we did it there he tried to come back. Later on I went back when I was a student at the Academy to play the organ in *Noye's Fludde* and they came to that, but during that period I didn't see much of them both, which also meant that I wasn't in close contact with what was being written at that time.

By late 1953, Lesley was spending much less time with Britten and Pears. The reasons aren't obvious. She had almost disappeared from the concert circuit and was now teaching singing at a convent school. Had she finally become one of Britten's 'corpses'? Those who got too close often found themselves cast aside after their allure or usefulness had faded. Apparently not, for while she was no longer in the inner circle, there's no evidence of any hostility from Britten or Pears, and she still felt comfortable enough to approach them for advice. But by this point, Imogen Holst, a musicologist and occasional composer, the daughter of Gustav Holst, had taken up residence in Aldeburgh for good, to assist with the administration of the Aldeburgh Festival. She was to be Britten's music assistant from 1952 to 1964. Her presence might have done something to dislocate Lesley's relationship with the two men. Whatever it was they sought from devoted women was in ample and local supply. Any more might have been overwhelming.

In November, Lesley went to a performance of *Peter Grimes* at Covent Garden. Pears was singing the title role and Reginald Goodall was the conductor. Britten, suffering with bursitis, had his arm in a sling, and struggled with letter-writing. His customary thank-you letter to Lesley for his latest birthday present – a volume of the writings of Epictetus – was typed. At least Steuart appeared to be feeling better:

> I had a nice quiet birthday, without Peter alas, but with some nice young ones, which of course pleased me! I saw you in the distance at P.G. the other night, and was sorry not to be able to attract your attention. It is such ages since we met. Perhaps next time I'm up you can visit me in Chester Gate (with Stewy?) because the doctors are pretty strict about me going about.
>
> Please forgive the horrid typing but my left-handed writing is still rather obscure, although it's improving – music is much easier than words I find. There isn't much improvement in the arm yet, but we are still hoping. I'm so glad that Stewy is at last better. What a horrid time it has been for you all. Please tell him I will answer his nice p.c. [postcard] very soon.

A few days later Britten sent a postcard to Steuart, scrawled with his left hand: 'Thanks for your nice birthday letter. I am so glad you are better. *I* can't use my right arm yet – as you see!'

Britten and Pears visited the Bedfords for supper during the Christmas holidays, when Britten played some of Beethoven's Fourth Concerto to

Steuart with just his left hand. In February of the following year, 1954, Pears sang *Saint Nicolas* at Lancing, with Steuart in the choir, and Pears signed his score. At last, Steuart was beginning to share his mother's enthusiasm for Britten as a composer:

◊

I THOUGHT *SAINT NICOLAS* was a wonderful piece. I loved that. But the moment when I realised Ben's genius as a composer? That would have been *Albert Herring*, when I first worked on it in 1960. That would have been when I really realised. It's later than you would have thought. But that's when I first really got to know an opera. That's been with me all my life, that piece, and funnily enough when I came to work on it, I sort of knew the tunes. I sort of knew how it went, but I don't quite know how, because I'm sure I never saw a performance in the early days, when my mother was singing in it.

I spent a lot of my school period being not very well, missing terms – and there was one time he sent me some scores of his stuff. He sent me his *Diversions*. He sent me a copy of his Piano Concerto with a note in it that said, 'Hoping to hear you play it in September.' Well, of course, I wasn't up to it then and it's been one of the great regrets of my life – one of the many regrets of my life in this particular relationship – because I could have learned that piece when I was a student at the Academy, but I got dragged onto other things. So it was *Albert Herring* that really got me going.

◊

In September 1954, having recently turned fifteen, Steuart was seriously ill again, and again he was alone and bedridden at home, this time for most of a school term. The illness of two years before had left him with chronic colitis. This meant that for the rest of his life he would be faced with periods of remission but also with the absolute certainty of the disease's occasional return. He had developed terrible acne too, and so-called 'moon face', both symptoms of Cushing's syndrome brought on by the regular doses of steroids he was receiving. It was a heavy burden for a young teenager and it took its toll.

◊

ONE OF MY EARLIEST MEMORIES was sitting in bed – again in one of my ill periods – listening to the first broadcast performance of *The Turn of the Screw* from Venice and that caught me. I was fascinated by that. I remember listening to that first performance, and *A Midsummer Night's Dream* when that was broadcast as well, in 1960. There were always tunes you could remember from his first performances, even though that was the first time you were hearing it. There was something you could catch onto.

◊

In his solitary confinement, Steuart played the piano as often as he could manage, and while his heart was set on becoming an organ scholar, his ability at the keyboard meant he was soon learning the great Romantic piano concertos. But he became withdrawn and depressed, a pattern that would continue for years to come whenever the illness recurred.

In the new year of 1955, while in remission from colitis, Steuart took his first skiing holiday, on his own. Like his mother, he felt buoyed by the mountains, both in winter and summer, and would return often over the next twenty years, usually on his own.

At Lancing, he was finally able to take regular organ lessons. He played for the odd chapel service, giving full recitals by the time he left. This, despite his last three years at Lancing being plagued by frequent relapses into illness. When he was sixteen, he interrupted one of these bouts of colitis to play the first movement of the Schumann Piano Concerto with the school orchestra. He left the sanatorium in the afternoon, played the rehearsal and the performance while the school doctor hovered on standby in the wings, and then promptly returned to his sickbed.

The next year he played the virtuoso piano part in Constant Lambert's *The Rio Grande*, and in his final term, aged still only seventeen, the first movement of Rachmaninov's Second Piano Concerto. His contemporary, Sebastian Kraemer, described it as 'very exciting!' Kraemer says of Steuart, 'Even as a teenager he had the same personal style as when I last met him about ten years ago; really engaging and charming, in a grumpy, conspiratorial way.'

In Field's House, Steuart's study was next to a mural by Edward Piper, later a professional artist, who was in the year above. With Britten's 'rather eccentric' nephew, Sebastian, also at Lancing, the school had become a magnet for Aldeburgh-associated offspring.

In 1957, Steuart joined the Royal Academy of Music and immersed himself in London's musical life by going to as many concerts and operas as he could afford. His pocket diaries are full of *Falstaff*s and *Figaro*s at Covent Garden or Sadler's Wells, recitals by Dietrich Fischer-Dieskau, concerts and Proms. He returned to Lancing to play the organ in *Saint Nicolas* – again with Pears as the tenor soloist and Britten in the audience – and also in *Noye's Fludde*, just a year after its first performance. He played for the occasional opera rehearsals at the RAM, including many for *Albert Herring*, but still he harboured absolutely no ambitions to conduct.

For Steuart's nineteenth birthday, his father Leslie bought him a motorbike that had to be collected from Austria. So Steuart flew over and rode it back via Salzburg, Munich and Brussels, stopping to hear operas and concerts. He fell off just outside Calais and injured his leg, but persevered across the Channel and home. Two years later he was back in Salzburg again, and in Oberammergau and Munich. In the course of that one holiday he saw *Falstaff*, *Capriccio*, *Die Meistersinger*, *Arabella*, *Don Giovanni*, *Le nozze di Figaro*, *Der Rosenkavalier*, *Ariadne auf Naxos*, *Die Zauberflöte* and *Intermezzo*.

Following his childhood ambition, Steuart applied to become organ scholar at King's College, Cambridge, but after a lengthy trial was pipped to the post by John Langdon – a protégé of David Willcocks, the newly

LANCING COLLEGE CHAPEL

SAINT NICOLAS

A Cantata

Music by BENJAMIN BRITTEN

Words by ERIC CROZIER

*This Cantata was written for performance at Lancing's
Centenary celebrations in 1948.*

THE LANCING COLLEGE CHORAL SOCIETY

THE CHOIR of the BRIGHTON & HOVE HIGH SCHOOL FOR GIRLS

With representatives of The London Choral Society

Saint Nicolas - PETER PEARS (O.L.)

Young Nicolas - Christopher Morgan

The Pickled Boys - James Oldham
Christopher Coldham
Nicholas Pattison

Organ - Steuart Bedford (O.L.)

Piano Duet - Christopher Headington & Antony Saunders (O.L.)

The Gallery Choir conducted by Josephine Dalmaine

Leader of the Orchestra - ELUNED CHAPPLE

Conductor - JOHN ALSTON

Sunday, 1st June, 1958

*The Cantata will be preceded by a performance of
"A Hymn to the Virgin" (Benjamin Britten), given
by the Lancing College Choir.*

appointed Director of Music at King's. Massively disappointed, Steuart accepted instead an organ scholarship at Worcester College, Oxford. On the plus side, the duties were much lighter than at King's.

Meanwhile, his brother Peter was now thirty and making modest headway as a singer under the professional name of Peter Lehmann Bedford. David had married at the age of just twenty-one and had two infant daughters. He was supporting himself and his family by working as a music teacher while developing his career as a composer. To the dismay of his parents he was also a regular on the Campaign for Nuclear Disarmament's Aldermaston marches and protests, where the threat of arrest was perpetual.

In June 1961, shortly before Steuart graduated from the RAM, Lesley wrote to Britten. He was hoping to help out another young man, Peter, an eighteen-year-old musician who was looking to make a start in London, and had turned to Lesley, probably in the hope that she could put him up. Her reply gives us a glimpse into the Bedford household.

I have my sister & husband & children coming from Africa in July – they will only be here for a short time (i.e. in this house) but it uses up all the rooms – also Steu has his final diplomas at RAM & would be on the piano practically non-stop. But come September or Oct the way will be clearer. Steu takes up an organ scholarship & will be away and though it's a rather haphazard sort of household and the room nothing of the Ritz, there it is, and the pianos of course and all one could do to leave him alone & yet make him happy!

[. . .] I could with little difficulty find a room in one of the houses rather 'given over' to students. [. . .] Or would you like me to try & find somewhere like that straight away with the thought that if it doesn't work he can come to us in the autumn? [. . .] If he was in this sort of place he could always weekend here when Dave & babies are always with us & a good deal of noise & affection & muddle.

Who is he with for piano? [...] I am only thinking aloud at this moment of Steu's teacher Henry Isaacs, not perhaps a very great teacher but a wealth of understanding of concerts shared, of parties in his studio, of students playing to each other. This is the sort of life which I feel he should be in the middle of. Well, these are just thoughts Ben dear. [...]

Steu is giving us anxious days again – after these years the trouble starts up again. Perhaps he will have it all his life but he accepts it all wonderfully. As for Dave thank goodness there's another Aldermaston over without getting himself arrested. It is all one can say!

Steuart was no longer Stewy, but for a while at least, Steu, and it was at Oxford that he realised that he might not be cut out for the life of an organist after all.

When I went to Oxford I thought I was going to become a cathedral organist. I was very unambitious in that way. I was quite a respectable organist, though I say it myself, so I could have easily taken up a post in a good church, then graduated to a cathedral, and that would have been a nice sedentary occupation. But it became apparent – after working with the choir at Worcester College, and having worked with the stuff that I was required to do – that I couldn't live my life on just the music in the regular church repertory at the time. A lot of it was very nice, but it occurred to me that I wasn't going to be able to live with this for the rest of my life.

His contemporary, David Kimbell, remembers Steuart's music-making:

In chapel, at his first Christmas service, the first outing for Messiaen on the college organ (amiable consternation of the college chaplain); Liszt's *Via Crucis* (a work from which I have ever since taken evasive action); otherwise a heroic embrace of a wide liturgical repertory with an exceedingly modest bunch of singers. We all assumed, and I think he half did himself, that he would be heading off to some cathedral close when he left Oxford. Outside chapel it was his piano playing that made the mark, and the exceptional discipline that enabled him to find time to master and extend his already extensive repertory: really big pieces like the Rachmaninov Third Piano Concerto, the Schumann Fantasia in C and so on. He also had a number of 'preposterous' (the vogue epithet at the time) party pieces: the Godowsky arrangement of Chopin études for instance.

Steuart started to play for the University Opera Club – accompanying a complete performance of *The Rake's Progress* at the piano – and performed several times as a concerto soloist with various university orchestras. In his first year he played Beethoven's Fourth Concerto, and in his second, Rachmaninov's Second and Third Concertos, in short succession, at the Town Hall. A few months later he was giving an organ recital at Westminster Abbey. He kept up with Britten a bit. He saw *A Midsummer Night's Dream* at Covent Garden in 1962, and played for *Canticle II: 'Abraham and Isaac'* and *Noye's Fludde* (again at Lancing, with Britten there).

And then, for the first time, he conducted something that wasn't written for a chapel choir:

◊

THE UNIVERSITY OPERA CLUB used to put on a big production in the Christmas term and a minor production in the spring term. It's actually a very distinguished organisation – its history and the number of fascinating things they've done in the past. Whoever was going to conduct the 'minor' opera pulled out for some reason. The post became vacant and I nipped in there. I suppose my knowledge of the Britten and Pears scene helped a lot in securing that, because they'd already decided they were going to do *Albert Herring* in the Oxford

O.U. OPERA CLUB

presents

ALBERT HERRING

A Comic Opera by BENJAMIN BRITTEN

Libretto by ERIC CROZIER

Settings designed by STEPHEN WILKINS

Directed by RICHARD HUGHES

Conducted by STEUART BEDFORD

Playhouse, in the year it was refurbished, 1964. All the Oxford dramatic societies were invited to contribute one production, including us.

Of course, I'd already played *Herring* at the Academy, so I knew the score. When I auditioned for it, they made me stand outside the door and wait while they made up their mind. I think it was also known that I knew Ben and Peter, so as far as the publicity side went I'm sure they thought, 'Great, we're going to get Britten and Pears to come to the show!' It didn't quite work out that way but Ben did send me a telegram to wish me luck. It said: 'VERY SORRY CANNOT BE WITH YOU ALL BUT BEST OF LUCK AND BOUNCE ME HIGH. LOVE BEN AND PETER.'

I had done the *Serenade* before *Albert Herring* – that was the first Britten I conducted, in 1962 – but *Herring* was the first opera I ever conducted, in 1964. Oxford was where I caught the conducting bug. It was also when I really learned Ben's genius as a composer.

I wouldn't have known exactly what it was that appealed to me at the time, but looking back, first of all, it's one of the few comic operas in the English language. I can't think of another one of this century or the twentieth century. I can't think of another English comic opera, period, I would say, of such inexhaustible humour. But it's not just the humour of it. *Herring* contains serious music. As Ben always said, 'No comedy is of interest unless it is essentially about something serious', and there's a lot of serious stuff in *Albert Herring* as well.

Later on I managed to go through virtually all of the operas with Ben in one form or another – work through them – and it just struck me back in those days that it's an entirely delightful, brilliant piece, and the brilliance in it appealed to me. It's a virtuous piece in every way. Its virtues are for the orchestra, for the singers; and what he does with those forces is quite extraordinary.

But meanwhile, away from the opera, I had my duties at Worcester, where I had full charge of the choir and chapel services. This was quite a responsibility, even on the mornings when I overslept and missed the odd 8 a.m. service. Otherwise I was generally a very conscientious student and well behaved; though I was caught by the Dean flouting 'Women's Hours', which is surprising, as I was terribly behind in that department. And one night I was nabbed by a police constable who caught a bunch of us skinny-dipping in the River Isis after a night at the pub. The bobby yelled at us, we grabbed our things and ran for it.

Jack Westrup was my professor – an extraordinary man – and I suppose I did pretty well. I got a First in Music.

◊

David Kimbell remembers:

> … outings on Steuart's famous motorbike, a pre-war Austrian Puch, astride which on Saturday evenings excursions might be made into the Oxfordshire countryside. But no one college friend could count on pillion priority when there might be lovelies from Lady Margaret Hall or St Hilda's also hoping for a ride. My own pillion career culminated in our expedition to the south of France in 1963. We were at one point flown past by a new super Citroen of a kind which, Steuart informed me, Ben had recently purchased himself.

Uncertain as to what to do next, his health still an issue, Steuart decided to stay on at Oxford as a postgraduate, where he could live in college, eke out his tiny stipend with bits of concert work, weddings, funerals and organ recitals, and wait to see what would turn up. He was now twenty-five.

Yoxford, 2018

I have just tried to flush the lavatory but the chain has simply gone limp and nothing is happening.

Both of the lavatory cisterns in Steuart's and Celia's house are of the old-fashioned type, set six feet from the ground, connected to the bowl by a long brass pipe, and flushed by pulling on a lengthy chain. Steuart maintains that no other type of loo is worth having because only these have a strong enough flush 'to sweep all the crap away'.

I try the chain again. Nothing. Being a bit of a dab hand myself at light plumbing – another reason Steuart and I get along – I stand on the loo seat, lift the top off the cistern, and notice that the eye of the lever that pulls up the flush mechanism on the inside has sheared through. Which, if you are not a dab hand at light plumbing, probably makes no sense whatsoever. Suffice it to say, a bit of the loo has broken. I reach inside the cistern, flush, wash my hands, and go back to the kitchen.

'I'm terribly sorry but the loo has just broken.'

'Oh Christ!' says Steuart, his brow furrowing. 'What have you gone and done now?'

'I've had a quick look. The eye of the flush lever has corroded and sheared through.'

Celia breathes deeply and realises she has something urgent to do in another room.

'What? I don't think so. That seems highly improbable. I suppose I better have a bloody look.'

And Steuart shuffles off to the workshop in his cellar. He's seventy-eight, but Parkinson's or no Parkinson's he's going to get the stepladder out and fix it.

I set about trawling the Internet for the replacement part he needs – a lever and fulcrum apparently – and by the time I've found one (£2.99 including postage and packing) he is up the ladder, chuntering away to himself, the air blue with a Harewood-esque selection of swear words, making a repair with an old hose clip and a piece of string.

'Ooh. Couldn't you use a cable tie to do that?' I suggest.

'A cable grip? No, no, don't be silly, sod that.' He tightens a screw. 'Shit. Bloody thing.'

He tries the flush. It works, but there's now a worrying flabbiness to the operation.

'Hmm, well, that will have to do.'

'I can order the replacement part now, if you want. Apparently you need a lever and fulcrum.'

'A lever and a what? A fulcrum? What on earth are you talking about?'

'A fulcrum. It's the bit the lever sits on. It clips onto the cistern.'

'A fulcrum? I'm not so sure about that.' And he takes down the stepladder which bangs against the door frame.

'Agh, shit. Bloody thing.'

Celia makes us a cup of tea. There are biscuits too, which always act as a balm, and she knows that.

After a few biscuits Steuart says, 'Well, I suppose you better order that thing. The lever and the . . . what's it called?'

'Fulcrum.'

'Ridiculous. How much is that going to cost?'

'Two ninety-nine.'

'Hmm, well, that's not too bad. I suppose you'd better order it.'

SEVEN

I must go elsewhere, I must find a clearer sky, a fresher air

Steuart didn't have to spend much longer at Oxford.

In his first term back, the English Opera Group paid a visit to the Oxford Playhouse, bringing *The Turn of the Screw* and *Albert Herring*, just nine months after Steuart's own performances in the theatre. He wrote to Britten:

> Have you any idea which nights you will be conducting when the English Opera Group visits Oxford next month?
>
> I am sorry to trouble you at such a hectic time but I would be awfully grateful to know. The advance publicity gives no information on this point and I am most anxious not to book for a performance which, however admirably directed, is bound to lack the authentic touch!
>
> Is there any chance of seeing you when you come? I hope so.

Britten conducted two performances of *The Turn of the Screw* and Steuart went to them both.

I saw Ben after the first performance and told him I was also coming to the second, which was going to have a slightly different cast, including April Cantelo as the Governess.

I said, 'Can I take you out for a cup of tea before the show?'

'I'm afraid I can't,' he said. 'I have a rehearsal before the show.'

'A rehearsal? But how can it possibly get any better?'
'Oh, it can *always* be better!'

Albert Herring was conducted by Bryan Balkwill. 'But not very well,' according to Steuart. In a letter to Pears, Britten described Balkwill as 'pretty dreary'.

At the start of 1965, Steuart conducted Menotti's *The Consul* for the Opera Club. The evening after the last performance, he played the Second Brahms Piano Concerto, and two months later he stopped work on his thesis and left Oxford. Thomas Armstrong [Principal of the Royal Academy of Music, 1955–68] had offered him a professorship back at the Academy, an offer made even more tempting when John Streets, the Head of Opera, asked him to conduct some productions in his department. And he secured some work at Glyndebourne, where his mother had worked with Britten in the 1940s, as a répétiteur and music assistant.

I left for Glyndebourne in the summer term. My college rather approved of someone actually going out and getting a job, rather than sponging off the university.

I'm not naturally very ambitious. It's not in my nature to go dashing after slices of work, so I went to Glyndebourne to join the music staff and I thought I'd see how it developed from there.

I did the first season and then got rather ill, so I was taken off for a bit.

This is something of a Bedfordesque understatement. The colitis was back, and with a vengeance.

Despite repeated visits to Francis Avery Jones, his gastroenterologist, Steuart's old illness had become critical again. Again he missed the first term – this time of his new post at the Royal Academy of Music. By the end of 1965 he was desperately ill, and while Avery Jones was away and thus unavailable, and with surgery the only option to save his life, Steuart was admitted for an ileostomy – a daunting and difficult prospect for any young man. The operation was 'slightly botched', making the prospects of reversing the ileostomy very slim. Steuart's depression returned. Lesley turned to someone she had met and talked to in times of distress, Margaret Sampson.

◊

MARGARET WAS THIS REMARKABLE WOMAN. She wasn't trained as a counsellor or as a therapist; I'm pretty sure of that. But she had this natural knack of getting you to talk to her, of making you feel better. She was a bit of a life-saver. She used to come to the house and we would talk. I kept in touch with her over the years and she helped me a lot, getting over bouts of illness and total depression. After my operation, she helped me. I couldn't get going at all – I was aching all the time. She sorted that out, just through counselling.

I told Ben about her when he was having difficulties, just before we started the recording of *Death in Venice* in 1974. He was feeling blocked and depressed, largely because his heart operation had also not gone to plan. He felt he couldn't compose. So I persuaded her to go and talk to him. I took it very gently with Ben, of course. I said, 'You might find it very helpful.' It's a difficult subject to broach, so I just told him about my experience. I think they spoke about three times, at the most.

Peter, being the torch-bearer and protector, didn't approve unfortunately. He felt it was an intrusion, so she couldn't go very far. I took her down to Aldeburgh, and driving back we talked about it all the way, but I cannot remember how it went. I did say to her that she would find there are people who will not approve, and she said, 'Oh yes, I've already met the one!' She told me that Ben had written her a long letter in his own hand, which was very unusual, as after 1973 they were usually typed.

◊

In 1975, Margaret Sampson wrote a short letter to Britten in which she said she was delighted to hear that he was working again, 'for this confirmed my belief that you were experiencing a temporary withdrawal of this gift. I hope this fulfilment has increased. I know your physical condition continues to be a problem, but my desire was that you could be helped to accept its limitations. You have been daily in my thoughts and meditations and I continue to seek help and inspiration on your behalf.' If Britten showed Pears the letter, which seems unlikely, it's hard to imagine that Peter held much truck with its contents.

In early January 1966, within days of the operation, Steuart was accompanying his brother Peter in the London premiere of Britten's *Songs and Proverbs of William Blake*, in the Arts Council Rooms. The cycle had been heard for the first time only six months before, in Aldeburgh, sung by Dietrich Fischer-Dieskau accompanied by Britten himself.

Coincidentally, Britten too was suffering from intestinal problems and facing surgery of his own. Pears wrote to Lesley from Hamburg:

I didn't know that Stewie had been desperately ill, and therefore I had made up my mind that come what may I would be at the Family Concert at the Arts Council Rooms. Alas! 'Come what may' came – Ben went to hospital that day and I had to put in an extra rehearsal that evening. I was awfully disappointed, and I do hope you all had a nice concert without me – but I still wish I had been there.

Ben has an ulcerated and infected Diverticulum (an unnecessary pouch in the intestines, I think), and has to wait until it is less poisonous and then have an operation – two weeks in hospital and six weeks to recover – 3 months in all – uncomfortable and painful in several ways – but it may be the cause of a lot of past trouble, and they think it's right to remove it. We are assured that it is not malignant. Let's hope.

In her reply, Lesley wrote:

We had been so very worried over not knowing anything about Ben's condition. It was so good to hear this anxious and unhappy news – poor dear Ben – we long for it to be over for him. Perhaps no one knows better than we what it all involves through our experience with Steu. He had years of fighting a losing battle and his time at Oxford was dogged by worsening attacks (in spite of which he got a 1st!) then there was a crisis when we simply had no choice but the full-scale op and a pretty hair-raising affair it was too. But as always there were some wonderful compensations – great skill and devotion – all the things one fears are lost in the world.

The concert was his first appearance and his study of the Blakes in bed were of terrific therapeutic value! He's at the RAM now and conducting *Lucretia* in March! He has matured enormously through all this and is coping with a disability with the greatest skill and patience and humour. They say – like Ben – that he will be better than he has been in years and I believe this will be so.

A few days later, Britten wrote to Lesley from the Red House in Aldeburgh, where he and Pears had been living since 1957:

I was very touched by your sweet letter & thoughts. It is a wearisome time, but once the op is over, it'll be easier to take!

I was so sorry to hear about Stew – I had no idea since I was told he played the Blake magnificently. Give him my love and best wishes please.

It's a short note from Britten, but significant. He was aware of Steuart – how much he had overcome to play Britten's music, but also how well he had played his music in spite of that. He can only have been impressed and filled with enormous empathy for his fellow sufferer.

At the Royal Academy, one of the productions that John Streets asked Steuart to conduct was *The Rape of Lucretia*, as Lesley had mentioned to Britten in her letter.

He asked me to conduct it on the grounds that it was a 'family piece', he said, because my mother had been in it. And so I did that and it was very, very successful. We sort of built the Academy Opera Department up together. It became very interesting, with lots of interesting things to do – Copland's *The Tender Land*, Poulenc's *Les Mamelles de Tirésias* . . . I was doing quite a lot there. I enjoyed my time at the Academy. But when I went on the professorial staff, they started giving me classes to do as well – Sir Thomas Armstrong decided I should do this – and so I was really quite busy, but my main thing was conducting opera performances with their department.

In the spring of 1966, Steuart returned to Glyndebourne as one of the music staff.

◊

THEN SOMETHING VERY INTERESTING happened. The English Opera Group was holding auditions in the Crush Bar at Covent Garden, and one of the singers from Glyndebourne asked me to play. So I went up to Covent Garden and when I got there, there were dozens of other singers from Glyndebourne there as well, some of whom were extremely good. And they made me play for them too. Virtually all of them actually. Martin Penny, the official répétiteur, had a wonderful time off.

At the end of the auditions, despite the fact I hadn't gone there looking for a job, Colin Graham [the director of many of Britten's operas including the Church Parables and *Death in Venice*] – who was sitting there quietly – said, 'Can I have a word?' So we went into an office and he said, 'We would very much like to have you join us on our music staff. Ben would like to have you in the fold.' So, as they were offering to pay twice as much as Glyndebourne, there was no question. I joined, and that dictated the future course of my life.

Ironically, I got a job as an accompanist and none of the singers did. Not one of them!

I don't know how they'd heard of me. Obviously Ben must have been keeping a careful watch out for me as a possibility for the company. I've never discovered how much, but there must have been something of that sort. Keith Grant ran the Group from within Covent Garden, but Ben was still its guiding influence.

They offered me various things to do, including conducting *The Beggar's Opera* in 1967, the next summer at Sadler's Wells, and at the Expo '67 World's Fair in Montreal, my first trip across the pond. As far as I know, no one from the Group had ever seen me conduct anything at all.

Very soon after that, out of the blue, Ben rang my mother – I was still living with my parents – asking if I could be his assistant for the recording he was about to make of *A Midsummer Night's Dream*. That must have been an interesting phone call. My mother very rarely spoke to us about her time in the Opera Group with Ben, or even about our holidays in Snape. It wasn't a call I – nor she, I bet – was expecting at all.

You don't say no to that sort of opportunity, working for the very first time on a piece with its composer. So I presented myself at the Decca studios in West Hampstead. The Rolling Stones were recording in one of the other studios, but Ben didn't really have any idea who they were.

The first thing I did was coach the Rustics, and there was this wonderful cast, all lined up, ready for their first run. They had mostly performed it onstage, either in the original production at Aldeburgh or at Covent Garden, so they were more than familiar with their roles. But in the second act, when Bottom is telling the Rustics that someone – Snout, as it turns out – will have to play the wall, I couldn't help noticing that Owen Brannigan wasn't quite hitting the notes properly, so I sidled up to him and said that I thought he was a bit off the correct pitch. He just smiled and said, 'No, lad, them's not wrong notes. That's colouring!'

This was when I discovered an interesting thing about Ben. Surprisingly, he was extraordinarily reluctant to correct any of his singers. If they were doing it wrong, or if they were singing something wrong – the occasional pitch problem or rhythmic inaccuracy – or if he wanted it differently, he'd go at it in an oblique way. He'd say, 'Well, could you make it more angry or something?' In fact, what he was actually asking you to do was to sing the note values that he'd written, but he would never say that. When it came to rhythm, when he did want to make a correction, it would invariably be in roundabout terms that led the singer back to the printed note values, a process that had the distinct advantage of showing why he wrote it that way, not simply, 'I wrote this.' And if it was a singer of some renown, like, say, Alfred Deller, he would sprint to his defence. I said to him during the course of those rehearsals, 'Ben, he doesn't seem to be singing that appoggiatura on "Eglantine" . . . On the recording you won't hear it.' And Ben said, 'Oh, no, he does it but he does it very quickly!' Well, it wasn't there, I'm absolutely certain. And it was the same with Janet Baker, for instance. He never liked to say anything. For some reason there was some shyness there. It's as if he felt it was such an honour that a really distinguished singer was singing his music and he shouldn't really correct them. And so it was left for me to do it usually. And then if I tried to do it, he'd say, 'No, no, no, that's all right!'

It was the first time, as an adult, that I spent any length of time with Ben and Peter. Curiously, from that moment on, we never talked about our time together when I was a child. Nor did we ever discuss my mother or her time with the Opera Group. Not once. Ben still called me Stewy, until he was told by Colin Graham that I didn't like it any more, and he immediately stopped. Though, once, when we were having lunch at the Red House, I was offered some cheese and he said, 'Steuart doesn't like cheese', which was something he had remembered from when I was a boy. And he was right. I still don't like cheese.

◊

Steuart's contract with the English Opera Group was due to start in April 1967, and in the interim he was keeping busy. He coached Pears for his televised performance of Elgar's *The Dream of Gerontius*, conducted by Sir Adrian Boult. He conducted *The Rape of Lucretia* and *The Turn of the Screw* for the semi-professional London Opera Group, and *The Marriage of Figaro* and *The Magic Flute* at the Royal Academy.

His first job for the EOG was to be on the music staff for a new production of *A Midsummer Night's Dream*, directed by Colin Graham and conducted by Rudolf Schwarz. James Bowman, whom Steuart had known at Oxford as a lay clerk, was cast as Oberon. He too had been recruited from an audition at the Crush Bar the summer before. They rehearsed in Artillery House, in London, before the opera opened in Paris, with more performances at the Aldeburgh Festival in the newly opened Maltings, at Sadler's Wells, and on the Expo '67 tour in which Steuart was also to conduct *The Beggar's Opera*. In Paris they had to give two performances in one day, to work around a strike.

◊

BEN DROPPED IN to a rehearsal one day and there was definitely a heightened tension in the room. It was a very successful production, which the group revived again and again. James hadn't become his outrageous self, yet! The first year it was conducted by Rudolf Schwarz, which wasn't very good, and then Meredith Davies took it over for at least a couple of years. And then finally I got to take it over for a Snape and Sadler's Wells run in 1971, which was the first time I conducted it. I'd worked on it a lot, and played the celeste and harpsichord in the orchestra.

It's not an easy piece to do. In fact, one of the hardest orchestrally, and it's one of the hardest pieces to shape. It's a strange nod towards twelve-tone serialism. He never used serialism in the Schoenbergian way; he always did it his own way. He would just write four chords that would encompass the whole range. They would sound very weird, as in the opening of the second act, but that was his way of doing it.

There are so many different things you have to coordinate in that opera. Ben came to our final runthrough and was very helpful with his notes, as always. 'Don't do the final chorus any slower,' he said, meaning that it was getting too slow. I had, I am sorry to say, been enjoying it too much. He also wanted the Scotch snap in this chorus to be performed slightly faster, as if the crochet were made up of five quintuplets rather than four semiquavers. In the opening of *War Requiem* and in subsequent works he notates this precisely, but he didn't do this in earlier works.

During my first night in Snape, after Act I, Ben appeared in the wings. He didn't often stay to a whole performance, ever – I think he'd been rehearsing *The Turn of the Screw*. I thought, 'Good God, it's a bit early for me!' but he was very happy. I think he always knew that whatever he wanted, I would try and do. I think he had that confidence.

◊

Britten wrote to Steuart on 3 September 1971:

I stayed for most of Act II last night (until domestic pressures forced me home) & I was tremendously impressed & grateful for the way you handled it. I don't think I have ever heard the start of Act II so good, & the Rustics & Lovers' quarrel were brilliant! I am doubly disappointed that I can't come tonight. I am taking Peter over to our hide-out for 24 hours' break – but I expect to be back at any rate for the TV *Fludde* if not for a perf. tomorrow afternoon.

But heartiest congratulations on the way you made sense of & used those sketchy comments during the Dress Rehearsal.

From a very grateful composer!

Norma

'Steuart, we have to write something about Norma.'

Norma is Norma Burrowes, Steuart's first wife, and a very talented soprano.

I've been thumbing through Steuart's pocket diaries, trying to decipher the scrawled entries with him. They are not always helpful: '3 pm Ben' or '7 pm opera' is often the full extent of an appointment. Ben who? Ben Britten? Ben Luxon? Which opera? Where? On 16 June 1973, the world premiere of *Death in Venice*, his diary merely says, 'D in V. I'.

The diaries offer no insight into Steuart's private life. There are no hints at dinner reservations, visits to friends, family or in-laws. There isn't even an entry for his first wedding, let alone any clue as to where it happened.

Just a year or so ago, the scribbles in these diaries would have sparked a vivid and specific memory for Steuart, much in the way that a single chord or a couple of notes can elicit a chain reaction of responses in any music-lover. But while music can still do this for Steuart, he struggles now to grasp a moment from a diary entry and hold onto it. Memories flit and disappear almost as soon as they have arrived.

I ask about an entry in 1967 and he starts to describe events from a decade before.

'No, this is 1967, not 1957 . . .'

'Oh, *sixty*-seven . . . well, I was at school then. That's not much use.'

'No, that's *forty*-seven . . .'

'Are you sure? Oh yes, sixty-seven. *Sixty*-seven? What about it?'

We work in his music room, its walls lined with bookcases full of scores, arranged in a system that Steuart alone can navigate. We talk about such-and-such an opera.

'I'll show you.' And he gets up from his chair, keen not only to prove to himself, if not to me, that he can locate the score in question, but also to move and thus ease the nagging, chronic pain in his lower back and legs.

He aims directly for a spot where the score should be. It's not there.

'Now where the fuck did I put it?' he mutters. 'Who's been moving my stuff around?' And after a ten-minute search he finds it on the piano. His restless mind has him constantly re-exploring his repertoire, pulling music off the shelf, browsing for a particular passage, setting it down, and not remembering later that any of this has happened.

One day, I browse through his full score of Verdi's *Falstaff*, which he keeps alongside a facsimile of Verdi's manuscript. The facsimile is not decorative, nor a sentimental keepsake. He has been through the entire manuscript and used it to make corrections in the modern score. Also in his score he has painstakingly written an English translation under every single word of Italian text. It is an extraordinary testament to hard work and diligent preparation, the like I've never seen in any other conductor's scores.

'Do we have to write about my marriage to Norma?'

'Yes, we do, or people will think it's very odd.'

'Oh. I really want this book to be about the work.'

While this is true, I sense too that he feels that any discussion about his first marriage is a betrayal of his second. He adores Celia, and their two daughters Charmian and Jo, to the extent that any personal life, any relationship before this one is best forgotten.

Ironically, it is Celia who volunteers to fill in the gaps that Steuart has no desire to discuss. Also ironically, it is Norma who introduced Steuart to Celia, at Glyndebourne in 1975, where Norma was singing *The Cunning Little Vixen* and Celia was a company manager.

Steuart and Norma met while he was conducting her in productions at the Royal Academy, where she was a student. The very first time she saw him, as he left the orchestra pit, she asked a friend, 'Who's that gorgeous man?' They married in 1969, in Belfast, and worked together occasionally for the English Opera Group. Colin Graham saw her in Poulenc's *Les Mamelles de Tirésias* (conducted by Steuart), was impressed and hired her, and she became a regular feature at Aldeburgh.

'But our careers drove us apart,' Steuart finally reveals. 'We were hardly ever together.' They became so busy that in 1976 they spent just two months together.

In 1977 they had a brief holiday and decided to separate, though they weren't divorced until 1980. Britten, who was fond of Norma, never knew that the marriage had hit the rocks. 'He *hated* divorces,' Steuart says. 'So it's just as well he never found out.'

As for Norma, she remembers the recitals they used to give together:

We used to do a lot of recitals. Steuart was such a wonderful accompanist. We never really had to discuss things; we just knew what was right. After we broke up, I almost stopped doing recitals, and I certainly never found another accompanist like Steuart. I tried, but it was never quite the same.

Norma went on to be happily married to the tenor Emile Belcourt and had two children with him, as well as being a stepmother to his seven others. After Emile died in 2017, Steuart got back in touch and they have spoken several times since.

Steuart Bedford with Norma Burrowes, 1970.

EIGHT

How much better to live, not words but beauty, to exist in it, and of it

The 1967 Aldeburgh Festival was Steuart's first as a performer. As well as working on the music staff for the performances of *A Midsummer Night's Dream* in Snape Maltings, he found himself playing for a concert at the Jubilee Hall devised by Britten and Pears, 'Two Musical Families', which featured music from the seventeenth century by William and Henry Lawes, but also, and more significantly, music by Steuart's own family. He accompanied Margaret Cable in some songs by his grandfather Herbert Bedford, then played a piece by his brother David. Next on the programme was another song by David, which Peter Bedford sang, accompanied by Steuart and David. Finally, Britten played several songs by Liza Lehmann (Steuart's grandmother) accompanying April Cantelo, Margaret Cable, Peter Pears and Peter Bedford.

Pears wrote the programme note:

Liza Lehmann, the daughter of artistic and musical parents, made her debut as a soprano at the Monday Popular Concerts in 1885, at the age of twenty-three. It was a huge success and she rapidly became one of the most sought-after singers in England. Joachim and Clara Schumann had been her friends, and the latter, in her eighties, had accompanied her in Robert's 'Nussbaum' and 'Frühlingsnacht'. In 1894, on her marriage to Herbert Bedford, she retired from the concert stage and took to composing. A whole series of most successful cycles appeared, all written with great expertise and charm. The first cycle was *In a Persian Garden* (1894) to Fitzgerald's *The Rubáiyát of Omar Khayyám,* and from 1909 she toured England and America, accompanying a quartet of the best singers of the day, with enormous success. Just before her death in 1918 she finished a characteristic and charming biography, full of memories of the period. Here is one from the Art Nouveau days: 'I suppose I was intended to be flattered when a young lady of our acquaintance one day rushed up to me after a performance [of *In a Persian Garden*], saying, "Oh thank you! Thank you! *Do* let me thank you! The local colour is too wonderful. I *have* so enjoyed it – I simply felt as if I was at *Liberty's*!"'

Herbert Bedford had had some musical training at the Guildhall School of Music, though his family had insisted on his working in the City. He was an expert miniature portraitist, and very successful. His chief distinction was the winning of the Brahms Prize of the City of Hamburg, the first Englishman to do so. He composed works for the stage, orchestra and chamber music; but according to *Grove's Dictionary*, his most original compositions were for military band and for unaccompanied solo voice.

After some years at the Royal Academy of Music, David Bedford studied in Italy with Luigi Nono. His *Piece Two (Electronic)* was performed at Aldeburgh in 1963. He subsequently worked with Witold Lutosławski, and now tends to use more conventional instruments.

It is hard to imagine a stronger, almost paternal gesture of welcoming Steuart into the 'fold', particularly as he had no involvement whatsoever in the concert's planning.

◊

I'M SURE MY PARENTS both came. It must have been a very interesting experience for them, that concert. I don't remember them talking to Ben and Peter afterwards, but it's difficult to imagine that they didn't. Since my childhood, I can remember seeing my mother talking to Ben just once. They were having a very intense conversation in the foyer of the Maltings during the interval of a concert, but I never discovered what it was about.

She never talked to me about him, and he never mentioned her to me. I can't think of any other childhood friends who went on to become adult colleagues, but I could be wrong. It's as if they were two different friendships that weren't bound together.

Most people would say Ben was a tortured man but I didn't see that side. How many close friends did Britten have? Well, I think they're fairly easy to find. If I had gone to him with a problem he would have given me friendly support, but I did try to keep a safe zone. I didn't try to get too close. I think the idea that I too might get too close, get burned if you like, was something that terrified my mother. But I knew it was important, occasionally, to say no to offers of lunch at the Red House, to keep a slight distance.

◊

The main thing on Steuart's mind in the summer of 1967 was *The Beggar's Opera* and his imminent conducting debut at Sadler's Wells, just after the Aldeburgh Festival.

◊

DURING THE 1967 ALDEBURGH FESTIVAL I petitioned Ben to go through the piece with me. I didn't think he would because it was Festival time, a busy time for Ben. He was always on somewhere, doing something. Well, he did. Not only did he do it; he gave me two sessions and played the whole thing through with me, singing away in his gravelly voice. He played it through and talked about it, gave me the speeds and everything, and what to do and what used to happen when he did it. It was wonderful. He was always very generous about that sort of thing. If you said to him, 'Look, I'm doing your piece, have you got some time?', he'd always try and make it possible. He'd say,

'Come over to the Red House', and he would play and I would sit next to him at the piano in the library, the beautiful studio that had been converted from a barn, making notes in the score. Receptive ears could learn an enormous amount from the way he played his own music. Miss Hudson would bring tea or coffee. He'd just ring a bell and she would appear. I'd often stay for lunch afterwards, just the two of us. Unlike someone like Lennox Berkeley who really didn't care the slightest bit how his music was performed (to the extent that you wondered why on earth he wrote it!), Ben was fanatically interested in how his music went, and he expected people to do it the way he wanted it; which is why, apart from anything else, he wrote it out very clearly. And if somebody was interested in doing that, he would be interested too.

The problem with *The Beggar's Opera*, if it is a problem with the piece – certainly the thing that some people find difficult – is the fact that originally it was a play with music. Ben has taken it over so that it has become music with a play. The dialogue has become less important, and the music takes a much stronger role. This means you have to rethink how you play the dialogue. And in a large number of cases it needs to be shortened, otherwise you get both music and dialogue fighting with each other.

I remember when we first did it at Sadler's Wells, even though we used to cut it down quite a lot, it seemed to be a terribly long evening. But when I came back to it many years later, we did all the numbers and it wasn't long at all. And again, when we recorded it, it just didn't seem long in any way. I think this was largely because we'd shortened the dialogue quite considerably. I think that's what you have to do. Otherwise, it gets too long and the audience doesn't quite know what it's listening to.

All the arrangements in *The Beggar's Opera* have this wonderful appropriateness to the tune that they are underscoring. His accompaniments are not as in the Dudley Moore parody, 'Little Miss Muffet'.

That was a very clever idea but it presented Little Miss Muffet with an irrelevant accompaniment, or what was perceived as one, as it didn't have anything to do with the tune at all. But in fact Britten's accompaniments *do* have something to do with the tune, very much so. Everywhere you go, you can hardly turn without seeing some relationship. And the harmonies are maybe a little bit personal, shall we say, to Britten, but they are never ugly. Something like 'Over the hills and far away' is quite ecstatically beautiful; in every bar the winds contribute in some way until it all comes snaking down. It's extraordinarily beautiful and mellifluous.

He came to the dress rehearsal of *The Beggar's Opera* and gave me lots of notes. And everybody said to me, 'Oh, that's a good sign. It's if he doesn't give you any notes, that's when you want to watch out.'

I still have the notes, all in this ilk:

Less flute in 6/8 overture
More bassoon in Fill every Glass
Pretty Polly too fast.
Edie [Coates] start If any wench softer.

He was always asking singers to make more use of their soft singing. I was once sitting with him during a dress rehearsal of *The Turn of the Screw* when the Miss Jessel (usually a heavier soprano) started 'Here my tragedy began' rather fruitily. He groaned audibly. 'Can't she start it softer?' It is, after all, marked *pianissimo*.

Ben was either complimentary or not at all. Nothing. The general belief was that if he didn't say anything it was probably OK.

I never felt he was taking me under his wing. Never. One or two things that he liked that I did: he liked that I took a lot of trouble trying to get things right and organised. I was meticulous. He approved of that. He really wanted people to sing and play what he wrote. He wasn't very happy if they went off onto another track: 'I don't want anybody to interpret my music. I just want them to sing what's there.' And there is enough there to worry about.

The role of the conductor isn't just to manage what he's put on the page; you have to understand *why* it's there. That's the important thing. It's no good just saying, 'Do this accent, this staccato . . .' You've got to see why it's there, what he's trying to do, what word he's trying to point. It's not an encumbrance, which some people find it rather difficult to understand: 'Oh, it's cramping my idea of what it ought to be!' It's just *better* if you do it the way that he wants it. That doesn't mean that you're going to follow a direction slavishly – as long as you understand what it's doing there. You may find a perfectly acceptable way of creating the same idea.

I think it's possible I had an innate sense of that because of my family history with Ben. I don't know. It seemed very natural to me.

◊

Steuart's full professional debut with *The Beggar's Opera* was at Sadler's Wells on 15 July 1967. His brother Peter was in the ensemble, singing the small role of Jemmy Twitcher. That night, not far away at the Royal Opera House, Covent Garden, Joan Sutherland and Luciano Pavarotti were singing together in *La Fille du Régiment*, so the competition was stiff. Nevertheless, Steuart garnered a favourable review in the *Daily Telegraph*; though he likes to point out that the impressed critic, David Money, had also been Steuart's first piano teacher.

From that point onwards the professional relationship worked rather well, and very soon I was doing all sorts of other things, and we were getting through most of the operas.

In October *The Beggar's Opera* went with *A Midsummer Night's Dream* to Montreal for a hectic week of performances at Expo '67. Steuart returned to London for his duties at the Academy, and to conduct *The Barber of Seville* and *Così fan tutte* for the London Opera Group. In Cologne, he led the Melos Ensemble in a programme of music by Peter Maxwell Davies and Harrison Birtwistle, and even managed to squeeze in an organ recital in Cambridge. In December he was back in the recording studio with Britten, this time to assist him on *Billy Budd*.

◊

WE RECORDED IT at Kingsway Hall and I was responsible for the kids. They have only a tiny bit. There were two sections, the second of which is terribly short. They just have to sing, 'Ay Ay, Sir!' in the battle scene. Everything stops for that, practically. We were crashing our way through the scene – *This is our moment!* and all that – everybody was going at full tilt, all very exciting, and we got to the bit where the boys come in and . . . silence. I'd completely forgotten about it.

'How do I get out of this one?' I thought. So I blamed the boys. Terrible. A conductor blames the performers; that's a first.

It's awfully exciting that scene. Whenever I'm doing the battle scene, with the onstage drums, I just tell the players, 'You've got to hit the shit out of it.'

There were also bits of offstage music to do as well, and there were singers that needed help. Peter Glossop couldn't get the note for his last 'Starry Vere, God bless you!' He yelled down the microphone, '*Can I get the fucking note???*' Ben was quite shocked. So I said I'd give him the note. So I'd hum him the note, but he'd still come in a third too high. John Culshaw [who was producing the recording for Decca] came out and said, 'How are we going to get this right? Can we put a musical machine beside him?'

And Ben said, 'He's got a musical machine beside him. It's Steuart.'

I think Glossop got that wrong in the [1966 BBC Television] film too. Probably. I expect somebody was hiding behind a sail or something.

I had to keep an eye on the harps and xylophone too. For some reason they couldn't see the conductor. Quite tricky really.

Aldeburgh, November 2019

I arrive at Steuart's house for a session on the book. Since we started on the project, two major events have taken place.

Firstly, the Bedfords have moved house, from their Victorian manse in Yoxford, where Steuart's huge music library lived (along with his grand piano) in a converted coach house across the garden from the main body of the house, to a smaller house in Aldeburgh where the library, stripped of some excess fat, can live (again with the piano) in a sort of granny annexe on the ground floor. The thinking is that as Steuart's disease progresses his mobility will diminish, and eventually he and Celia can live entirely on the ground floor. It's a good house for this plan, which they hope will take a few years to come into its own.

The second event has proved the wisdom of the first decision. Steuart has had a fall, brought on by an imbalance in his medications. He is also suffering from bouts of nighttime confusion that leave him disoriented and anxious. So, after a three-week bout in hospital, he has returned home to a hospital bed in his library. He can almost reach his piano from his bed. Celia and a carer take it in turns to sleep on a Lay-Z-Boy chair in a corner. By day, Steuart is never happier than lying on his bed, listening to an old tape of *Beyond the Fringe* that has been unearthed during a clear-out of old boxes, in particular Dudley Moore's parody of Pears singing the Brittenesque realisation of 'Little Miss Muffet'.

As I come through the front door, I can hear the piano playing. Mozart, it sounds like. I walk the length of the house to Steuart's room, and there he is, playing beautifully. It's the piano part of a Mozart trio. I tell him it's lovely but he demurs. Not good enough. He is almost bashful, like a child who has been overheard as he practises.

And I think suddenly about the story he has told me of the time he played to E. M. Forster in the school hut. What an extraordinary sight that must have been: the grand old man of literature sitting on a wooden chair at one end of the hut, while the small, shy boy, his feet barely reaching the pedals, entertained him with some Mozart on the battered old school upright.

NINE

The power of beauty sets me free

The Church Parables were the only Britten operas the English Opera Group performed in 1968. Britten's health continued to be a problem. He spent most of January in Venice, composing *The Prodigal Son*, the last of the Parables, but within weeks of returning home was back in hospital – this time with the first signs of the heart issues that were to shorten his life. After severe flu symptoms, he was diagnosed with endocarditis and filled with enormous quantities of penicillin.

Ever the pragmatist, with the Church Parables Britten had found a way of writing new operatic works for the English Opera Group that required neither large resources to mount them, nor difficult opera houses in which to produce them. Best of all, being conductorless, he could spare himself the agony of having to perform them. It was a brilliant solution not only to the perpetual financial worries of the EOG, but also to his problem with nerves.

◊

MY MOTHER TOLD ME once, when Ben was downing some whisky before going on to conduct a performance, she had asked him, 'Ben, why do you do that?' He said, 'Darling, if I didn't do that, I'd never get up the stairs!'

He was a conductor who approached everything from the music. There was never any egotistical nonsense that you so frequently get – conductors wanting to show themselves off in the right sort of shirt or the right sort of gesture, or rehearsing their gestures in front of a mirror or something ridiculous. Everything was entirely music-orientated, and he endeavoured to get an orchestra to phrase the same way as if he was playing it on the piano. So his movements reflected this, and musicians – first-class musicians, which of course were those that he worked with – were able to pick up on this even if they didn't quite know how. I certainly didn't see quite how that worked. But it did and he was able to get some of the most remarkable performances, even though I couldn't totally understand how it worked. But all I did know was that it did work. That's one way, I suppose, of saying that from a professional conductor's point of view his technique was – how can I put it? – unorthodox. But nonetheless it worked and it worked for him. It didn't stop him from being horrendously nervous about it and I'm quite sure that that was part of the problem with his elbow, that he simply couldn't face conducting something.

◊

Steuart spent the start of 1968 skiing, before going to Baden-Baden to conduct the Melos Ensemble again. The concert was in a casino. Afterwards, Steuart and the players thought it would be fun to do a bit of gambling.

After the concert, as normal, we changed out of our concert garb and headed to the casino. But they wouldn't let us in because we weren't dressed properly. So we went back to the hotel, changed back into our concert wear, and headed straight back to the casino. I won quite a bit of money.

With the spring came some performances of *Curlew River* and *The Burning Fiery Furnace* in the King's Chapel in the Palace of Versailles. Steuart played the organ, and in the absence of a conductor, was the de facto music director. As with the other two Parables, Philip Ledger played the organ in the premiere of *The Prodigal Son* at that year's Aldeburgh Festival, and on the subsequent recording, while Steuart prepared the chorus of monks (among whom was his brother Peter). Once all three Parables were in the repertoire, Steuart was at the helm, and they toured frequently and extensively. In 1968 alone, the Parables went to Brussels, Edinburgh, Perugia, Padua, Berlin, Hamburg, Leverkusen, Düsseldorf, Darmstadt, Durham and Gloucester. On top of his weekly salary as a member of the EOG music staff, Steuart was paid an extra £15 per performance.

I escaped the smell of the tyre factory in Padua by taking a trip to Venice, the first time I had been. In Germany we had a nasty experience at the border – they wouldn't let us out of Berlin and we had a performance in Hamburg that night. So we had to rush to the airport and take a flight instead. Normally, we just toured in a bus.

We didn't get to see much of all these cities. We'd be off on the bus to the next venue straight after breakfast. Everyone was on the bus – the band, the chorus, the soloists . . . Ben Luxon, Bryan Drake, Osian Ellis, Jimmy Blades. Not Ben and Peter though, when they were around. Ben came very rarely, not even to revival rehearsals, and Peter sang only the occasional performance. Ben made a point of coming to *Curlew River*, when we did it at the Maltings in 1970. 'I was keen to see that people were keeping their standards up,' he said. He was always anxious over the performance of these works and often expressed his worry that the performers were becoming stale and routine, for him the ultimate blasphemy.

The band had to wear the full habits, sandals, all that, and in the early days we were inspected to make sure there were no trousers sticking out at the bottom. I got away with it actually – I just rolled up the bottom of my trousers and no one ever noticed. Once, when I hit the organ keys to play the first notes of the opera, absolutely nothing came out. I'd forgotten to check that the damn thing was switched on. Very unnerving.

We toured with our own chamber organ, which I used to have to tune too. That was always my entire afternoon taken care of. Luckily my father had invented a tuning machine, a sort of oscilloscope, which made it very much easier.

Two productions by the English Opera Group brought Steuart and Britten together in 1969: Mozart's *Idomeneo* and *The Rape of Lucretia*. This was also the year that the Maltings burned down on the opening night of the Aldeburgh Festival.

◊

I ASSISTED BEN when he conducted *Idomeneo*. And that was particularly interesting because I think I'm right in saying that apart from Purcell's *Dido and Aeneas* it was the only time Britten ever conducted an opera he hadn't composed himself. Moreover, it was his beloved Mozart. There was a tremendous amount to be learned from that. It was a wonderful experience. Ben approached it with loving care and reverence. Almost before anything else he called an extra rehearsal of the English Chamber Orchestra's strings to sort out the accompanied recitatives. This was very much a panic measure; it was the first time he had conducted anything like this. The orchestral parts were all marked with great precision as to phrasing and additional dynamics, and as the performance began to take shape, one was even more conscious of Ben's amazing breadth of vision, which contained a wealth of individual beauties.

I was there doing anything that was necessary, like playing a bass drum for the thunder, or cueing the monster on, or whatever I was required to do. When we came to televise it, I had to conduct the chorus most of the time, just to keep them together, because they were badly situated for seeing him. So it was a great experience and a major project.

It has been suggested that Ben chose *Idomeneo* as his first Mozart opera to conduct simply because it is one of the few Mozart operas that has a suitable title role for a tenor to sing, but I don't think it was that at all. It was a brilliant choice, and of course it was much less well known than the Da Ponte operas or *The Magic Flute*.

Unfortunately, that was the production for which the first night had to transfer from the Maltings due to the fire. On the Saturday night, we performed a couple of new operas in the Jubilee Hall – Gordon Crosse's *In Purgatory* and *The Grace of Todd*, for which I had to conduct the offstage chorus – during which time the fire started. I drove back to London that night completely oblivious. I didn't realise anything had happened. It wasn't until Sunday morning that my parents brought in the newspaper and said, 'Look at this. The Maltings has burned down!' It was in all the papers.

So I came back to Aldeburgh on the Monday, and after a couple of extra rehearsals, for which the ECO donated their services, we opened *Idomeneo* on the Tuesday in Blythburgh Church. It was a somewhat makeshift affair, and it wasn't until the following year that it could be seen in the setting and acoustic for which it was designed.

It's very interesting, though, the way this apparently frail man – or someone who appeared to be very frail and very nervous – was able to recover from these incredible reverses. Like the Maltings burning down. And I would instance the disaster of *Gloriana*. Most people would be absolutely knocked flat by that. With all that work and a major, major opera being performed and the reception that it got . . . But no, within a year he'd written and premiered *The Turn of the Screw*. His ability to recover from these reverses was quite extraordinary.

I should also mention Viola Tunnard, who was the main pianist on *Idomeneo*. Viola was a great friend of my mother. They used to do things together during the war, ENSA, that sort of thing. And I think she actually first got involved with the Britten set-up when she did some rehearsals for *Billy Budd* in 1951. She gradually got herself into Aldeburgh and then became a sort of a right-hand man for Britten in the actual assistance work.

Viola was hugely valuable on the Church Operas, a wonderful musician and an absolute perfectionist. Nothing was too much trouble – a really good, thinking, musician. She could be a strange character, and some people found her rather over-intense; a sweet person, but if things weren't going right, if you weren't 100 per cent on the ball, she could be very acid. Nonetheless, she was somebody whom you had infinite respect for. She was able to provide a tremendous amount of focus in a rehearsal.

Viola had a very difficult ending unfortunately, because nobody realised that she was suffering from motor neurone disease. She broke her leg, which didn't seem to mend – it turned out it was the first sign – and she became distracted and couldn't really concentrate any more. She was playing harpsichord for *Idomeneo* with Ben, and she was getting things wrong, which wasn't like her at all. Ben was going absolutely mad and couldn't understand what was going on. He didn't know what to do. And eventually he got rid of her, which was a terrifying event. He didn't know what had happened and when he finally discovered, it was too late.

This wasn't an unusual pattern. Eric Crozier – there was an interesting figure, another enigma. If you look at the libretto of *Albert Herring* you cannot escape the fact that it's a brilliant piece of work. It's masterly. From 1945, when he directed the original performances of *Peter Grimes*, to about 1951, he and Ben were inseparable. And then something happened, and I think this is almost a repeat of things that continued to happen, something went wrong somewhere, and Eric was simply discarded.

He told this to me many times: somebody once rang Ben when Eric was with him, and Ben eventually put the phone down and said to Eric, 'One of my corpses. You'll be one of those one day!' And Eric said, 'What an extraordinary thing to say to somebody.'

Of course it did in fact become true, and you never heard of Eric at all until the Britten–Pears School started in the 1970s and his wife

Nancy Evans was an important part of the singing faculty. That's over twenty years of being in the wilderness. And then Eric sort of reappeared, helping out with various bits of business at the School. Peter welcomed him back, particularly after Ben's death.

Eric could take offence at the drop of a hat. He just walked out. I'd seen him do it. We were working with him on an opera at the School and he just picked up his cases and went. The slamming doors that must have taken place when they first did *Albert Herring*! The original director was Frederick Ashton, who wanted to burlesque it all the time; that was absolute anathema to Eric. It would have infuriated him.

Eric was very touchy, and you did have to be careful. But on the other hand he could be incredibly generous. If you invited them around to dinner he'd come with baskets of jam and fruit, his latest book . . . everything, like a gift shop at Christmas. I'm almost certain he was manic depressive. I don't think he was ever diagnosed.

My mother was godmother to Helga, Nancy's daughter, Eric's step-daughter, and Helga used to tell my mother all sorts of things: 'Eric's gone and shut himself away and won't speak to anybody for three weeks' – that sort of thing. Which is characteristic depressive behaviour. And Helga, when she started having boyfriends . . . my God, they had a tough time if he didn't like them. He wouldn't sit in the same room with them.

And Montagu Slater, the librettist for *Peter Grimes*. He really couldn't cope with all the changes that were needed, so when Ben wanted something different he did it himself, or Eric Crozier wrote something, or Peter. And I suspect Joan Cross had a say in it too. So that libretto is probably the work of about five people. In 1946, Slater published what he considered to be his original libretto – *Peter Grimes and Other Poems* – and he said in his introduction, 'This *Peter Grimes* is what was sung at Sadler's Wells in 1945.' Of course it wasn't at all, and the whole of the mad scene had to be farmed out to Ronald

Duncan. If you compare that scene in the opera to Slater's original it's completely different.

Stephen Reiss was another of Ben's 'corpses'. He gave his life and soul to the Aldeburgh Festival, and managed to get people to come for thruppence-halfpenny. And even though he was General Manager, he would be the one putting out the chairs. He would fight for every last corner. Ben dedicated *A Midsummer Night's Dream* to him. He was a devoted and really delightful man. I played golf with him several times, and I'd always find him picking up my clubs and carrying them! But then it came to a disastrous end in 1971. Donald Mitchell disentangled the sorry sequence of events in his introduction to the third volume of Britten's *Selected Letters*. I think Peter in particular came to regret what had happened.

◊

The rest of the summer of 1969 was taken up by more performances of the Church Parables, a short run of *A Midsummer Night's Dream* in Bury St Edmunds, in which Steuart played the celeste, and a production by the London Opera Group of *The Turn of the Screw*, which he conducted at Sadler's Wells. Two months later, in October, he was back at Sadler's Wells, to share the conducting with Britten of the opera that had begun the Bedford–Britten connection twenty-three years earlier, *The Rape of Lucretia*.

TEN

Yet I am driven on

MY NEXT ASSIGNMENT with Ben was sharing performances of *The Rape of Lucretia* with him during the autumn of 1969. It was the first time Colin Graham's production had been seen in London, and the first professional production in London for many years. Ben was determined to give it its best possible chance, helped by an incredibly strong cast, including Janet Baker, Heather Harper, Peter Pears, Benjamin Luxon and John Shirley-Quirk. That was a delight, to work with that group.

This was the first time I assisted him on live performances of one of his operas, and I played the orchestral piano part too, when he was conducting. In a sense it was like a homecoming for me, after my mother's history with the opera. Funnily enough, though, that never, ever came up.

If you want to get to know an opera really well, there isn't a better way of doing it than sharing performances with the man who wrote it. How can you do better? Especially when the man who wrote it really knew what he wanted. And it was on that final run that he took particular trouble with that piece. He tried to get the libretto right. It was then when we did a few revisions, particularly the end.

We were rehearsing in Gower Street, and Ben was at nearly every rehearsal. It was very noisy sometimes, but just around the corner from Heals, and Peter arranged his diary to meet various people he wanted to see for lunch in the Heals restaurant. The waiter said he wished he had an autograph book.

One day we took Colin Graham with us – so it was Ben, Peter, Colin and me – and we took the score, and we rewrote the end, textually; sorted things out and tried to make it work, because the libretto has always come in for incredible stick. Everybody complains about it. I can't quite see why, but I suppose I can understand. Some people say they don't like having a sermon preached at the end, for instance. That seems to be a lot of rot. You can object to things like 'oatmeal slippers' and various strange, very Duncanesque lines. I contributed an alternative line to 'She had a restless night', which had always raised a few sniggers in the past. All these changes are in the later, post-1969 vocal scores, and do represent Ben's final thoughts on the piece.

It still amazes me that there were more than eighty performances of *The Rape of Lucretia* in its first year. It was written for a small ensemble – a cast of eight, and orchestra of twelve plus piano – that's twenty-one people in all, not counting the stage manager, of course. That's vastly different to something like the one hundred, at least, needed for *Peter Grimes*, which had come just before it. So the cost of *Lucretia* is so much lower, and you can take it almost anywhere. Britten felt that's where the future of British opera lay. But it wasn't what the critics wanted, especially with a rather risqué subject – the rape of Lucretia and all that. They wanted another *Grimes*, and it was totally, couldn't-be-more, different. So the reviews were pretty tough back in the 1940s.

I know Ben was desperate to make it work this time, because I'm sure he reckoned it was the last time he was going to conduct it. So, it was particularly interesting. He left me alone with the whole cast for a week, while he went on to something else, and was happy to leave me in charge. When he got back I said to him, 'Look, we've tried to sort out all the technical things.' And when he'd gone through it himself with them he said, 'Yes, I see that. But now we must let them relax.'

Peter always used to call me his Beckmesser. 'Oh, what have I done now? Oh, my Beckmesser!' Peter's words were notoriously alarming

– you never knew what he was going to sing. Ben said to me once, 'Look, please look after Peter, because you never know what he's going to say next.' And you didn't. This was an extraordinary thing. I mean, he could adjust, but sometimes it got away from him, like when he tried to say, 'Back, Collatinus!' instead of 'Back, Tarquinius!' In fact he got as far as 'Coll–' and he realised he'd said the wrong name, and said sort of 'Col-l-l- . . .' and stopped mid-word. Ben said afterwards, 'Peter tried to change the plot!'

I'm sure there was some sort of dyslexia, a mild form, because some of the things that used to happen could only be explained by a disjunction between word and thought.

After one of the rehearsals, Ben said to me of the big passacaglia at the end, 'Don't rush the finale. Let it breathe a bit.' So I duly did this, and when he did a couple of performances himself, he got to the passacaglia and he suddenly took off. Ben went like the clappers through it, really fast – faster than anybody had done it before. I don't know why.

◊

After hearing his dress rehearsal, Britten sent Steuart some notes. The musicians he mentions are Heather Harper (Female Chorus), Peter Pears (Male Chorus), Martin Penny (orchestral pianist), Philip Hooper (offstage quartet), Jenny Hill (Lucia), Janet Baker (Lucretia), James Blades (percussion), Osian Ellis (harp) and Peter Graeme (known as Timmy Crump, oboe).

Here, in great haste, are a few notes to give singers and players before Wed. evening, which you might include with yours.
F. Score
p. 10   Heather: Don't wait before 'from which Time fled'
68   Peter: ditto 'It is not far to Rome'
88   ditto   'Tarquinius knows no fear'
(I should rehearse 'linen' Trio, good as it was!)

145	Martin: find out what he did to cause that chain of disasters?!!
167	Philip (?) 'Now Roman *Masters*'
255	Jenny: dragged a bit here
267	Janet got out in the top line
271	If possible can she (Janet) wait for down beat in the last bar
293	Jimmy gets ahead with B. [bass] drum rolls in line 2
314 & 315	rehearse with singers
317	Osian: crescendo in bar 5 (not in part?)
325	I subdivided last bar & Timmy (oboe) didn't wait!

I may be on the late side for Wednesday's performance, but I will come and congratulate you at the end. Good luck!

A few days later, Britten wrote to Steuart after his first night. Robert Tear was on for Pears. It appears the cold and flu season was affecting the company. Bryan Drake, cast as Junius in *Lucretia*, was concurrently covering Owen Brannigan as Bottom in *A Midsummer Night's Dream*.

Sorry I had to desert you last night, but what with a day full of difficult meetings, & a streaming cold & sore throat (picked up from Peter or vice versa) I wasn't a fit companion for anyone. I heard most of Act I & it seemed to be going very well. Bob was doing fine & Janet didn't seem too tired. But what a fraught inauguration for you – though you seemed to be doing splendidly & the orchestra was playing well. I fear there may be new problems vis-a-vis Junius . . . but at any rate Peter is better. What a ghastly time of year!

The next summer, after a gruelling tour of Australia performing all the Church Parables – again for an extra £15 per performance – Steuart made his conducting debut with *Lucretia* at the Aldeburgh Festival. Pears was occupied with *Idomeneo*, which was finally making it onto the rebuilt Maltings stage, so Robert Tear replaced him as the Male Chorus. Otherwise the starry cast was the same as the year before. Steuart was also in charge of the chorus for *Idomeneo* and led *Curlew River* from the organ. Late in the day, he found himself propelled into the spotlight as a pianist. In an event billed as an 'Operatic Concert', Mstislav Rostropovich was due to accompany his wife Galina Vishnevskaya and the bass Mark Rezhetin in various operatic excerpts. At the eleventh hour, Rostropovich declared he would rather accompany just the soprano items, so Steuart was brought in to Cox and Box with the great Russian on the piano stool, and played for Rezhetin.

The English Opera Group's next major project, after a summer of more Church Parables, was Purcell's *King Arthur*. Philip Ledger conducted his own realisation of the score, and Steuart played the harpsichord. Norma Burrowes, Steuart's wife, was in the cast.

Philip Ledger was another conductor who was taking on a growing workload on the podium while Britten's diminished, though he too became aware of the pitfalls of succeeding too well. In his short memoir, *Memories of a Life in Music*, he wrote:

> In the 1968 Festival I conducted a semi-staged performance of *Hercules* by Handel at Snape [...]. Janet Baker sang the part of Dejanira that included an extended scene in which she goes mad. Her singing and acting were absolutely superb and at the end of the scene the audience erupted into a standing ovation. I had to wait for about eleven minutes before it was possible to continue conducting the piece. After the performance [...] the timpanist Jimmy Blades said, 'Well done, Phil! But remember, 5 per cent less than the boss!' He was absolutely right. Jealousy in its different forms is at the root of most problems. I was not in Ben's class as a musician and it was Janet Baker who had stopped the show. Was it then that the performance was a little too successful by comparison with performances given by Ben and Peter in the same Festival? Sure enough, when Peter reviewed the Festival events at the next Annual General Meeting he said, 'I suppose we have to say that *Hercules* was a success.'

Britten was not involved with *King Arthur* but Steuart soon found himself working closely with the composer on his next stage work, the television opera *Owen Wingrave*. The cast included Benjamin Luxon (Owen Wingrave), John Shirley-Quirk (Spencer Coyle), Heather Harper (Mrs Coyle), Jennifer Vyvyan (Mrs Julian), Janet Baker (Kate) and Peter Pears (General Sir Philip Wingrave).

◊

I WAS BOOKED as the assistant conductor by the BBC, presumably at Ben's instigation. All the music staff who were on that production – Amy Ward, Gordon Kember, Tom Gligoroff and I – went down to the Red House and played it through; either Tom or I played it through with Britten sort of demonstrating bits, but keeping quite calm. He didn't play it himself, and that's interesting because usually he did. And we just worked through it, and got the speeds, the feel of the piece, asked any questions . . . he was fine about that.

Then I had to spend a week in London with all the principals, just teaching it really, and learning it with them. And it was very hard, easily the hardest of the Britten operas from that point of view, of actually learning your pitches and coming in in the right place . . . very, very tricky. Indeed, we found that we were all struggling.

At the end of that first week, we had to go down to the Red House and sing it through with Ben, and I was rather nervous because I was sure they were going to get it wrong, which they did. But Heather Harper was extraordinary. She was a superb musician, and she'd missed the whole of that week's rehearsal – she simply wasn't available. So, Janet Baker, John Shirley-Quirk, Ben Luxon –everybody was struggling away to get the notes roughly right, and Heather Harper was singing the whole thing perfectly from memory, not having to open the score, note perfect, word perfect, and knitting at the same time, which didn't exactly endear her to the rest of the cast. Ridiculous. Janet seemed particularly irked, but we all laughed about it in the end.

The television recording was put together all in pieces and Ben, rather wisely, said he wanted to do a complete runthrough, with orchestra, in the Jubilee Hall first. Which we did. The whole opera, in the Jubilee Hall. We couldn't get into the Maltings because it was being set up for the recording.

When we were rehearsing the staging, just with piano, Peter had the idea of playing the General bow-legged, which we all found far too amusing for it to succeed. He was having his customary problems with the text, and in the dinner scene was making such a hash of it that by the 'scruples' ensemble everyone was giggling and it was falling apart. Jennifer Vyvyan was in the wings waiting to come on, but she caught the giggles too, screeched with laughter from offstage and simply failed to come on. Ben, who was rather oblivious to all this, stopped and said a bit tetchily, 'Where's Jennifer?' Peter saved the situation by saying, 'I believe she's changing her . . . linen.'

There were very few revisions during the rehearsal period, but the text of Owen's speech to the two ghosts was completely altered during one frantic lunch break.

Ben was not at all well. He was terrified of collapsing altogether, and he insisted on having me right beside him the whole time. Every so often I had to help out on the floor, because of the very complicated arrangement they had with the television. The whole of the Maltings was turned upside-down, with the orchestra on one level and loads of different rooms in the house at Paramore, all over the Maltings; some, miles away from the orchestra and conductor. There were some very tricky moments.

Ben was not in a happy mood at all, and really quite grumpy, particularly with the television people. It took a long time to record, almost a fortnight. We had to do most scenes several times. It's no wonder Ben was getting fed up.

There was one glorious moment when a monitor could not be fixed in the right place so that the singers could see Ben. They took an age to sort it out. It had to be hoisted up some nine feet in the air, then they had to hang it from the ceiling, and so on . . . It took forever, and when it was finally fixed he said, 'Good. Now we can get on with this bloody opera!'

You can see how *Wingrave* develops from the Church Operas. The percussion in the three Church Operas is very intriguing. It sort of builds from that. *The Prodigal Son*, the last of Church Operas, was 1968, and so when you get to 1970, all those techniques that he had used start coming into the main stage works, including this aleatoric business which you get in the Peace Aria in *Wingrave*, where the individual players have a degree of flexibility, playing groups of notes, and then come back together at the curlew sign, a notation symbol Britten devised when composing *Curlew River*. Sometimes it's not easy to arrange that. And there's the gamelan sound. He was clearly fascinated by it and of course it became a major, major feature in *Death in Venice*.

He never spoke to me about Schoenberg or Berg but did once confess himself to be pleased because he added something at the end of *Owen Wingrave*. It ends with this downwards sequence of notes, and that's the end; nobody sings anything. But then Peter suddenly decided he wanted to sing something. He felt the General ought to say something, to demonstrate some spark of humanity, and so Ben added three more notes at the end: 'My boy!' He said to me he was very pleased with this 'because it completes the row'.

It works perfectly musically, but unfortunately I have to say I disagree with it. He was pleased with the idea that it completed the row but dramatically I feel it weakens it. It's totally out of character. I simply don't believe the General would suddenly say, 'My boy!' The General is a hardened nut. Eventually Ben and Peter agreed with me, and when we did it on stage, for two runs at Covent Garden, I always talked Peter out of doing it. Annoyingly, it's still in all the scores. Anyway, if Ben could write a tone row in his own style, he'd be very happy about that.

Colin Graham, who didn't get on at all with Brian Large, the television director, said to Ben, 'What do you feel about this as a stage piece?' Ben replied, quite unequivocally, 'Do you seriously think that I would have written an opera just for television?'

Whether it worked as a television piece or not, he really reckoned it should work as a stage piece. Definitely. And I feel it does work as a stage piece. No opera can ever work on television, I've decided. First of all, it's the height of folly to commit a new opera to a television premiere. You're unlikely to have a reproduction system that is remotely comparable to a hi-fi system. In 1970 most televisions had just one, tinny loudspeaker. The other disadvantage is that television makes you look at a specific point. You're never allowed to watch the whole thing, as you can in an opera house, where you can take the bit you want to see. It's all there for you.

But Ben never saw *Owen Wingrave* on stage. Colin Graham said Ben would have changed it if he had seen it, but who's to know? We never really solved the end, in any production. I believe we should use a revolve for that. That's the music that to me requires a revolve so we can turn the thing around, but there it is. If Ben had seen it, that might have been one of the things he would have rethought.

It has been suggested that, at the end, Owen should tell the family to get lost but I don't think he would have rewritten to that extent. That would put a completely different slant on it. That would be like Captain Vere saying to Billy Budd, 'No, we won't hang you.'

One of the things about the piece that people have talked to me about – those who find it unsatisfactory – is they find that the family, the ones that are against Wingrave, are too cardboard-like. But I don't find this, any more than I find the village worthies in *Albert Herring* are cardboard figures. I didn't find this to be a satisfactory criticism because there were people like that in those days.

It remains, unfortunately, the runt of the litter, you might say. It's certainly not a view I would hold at all. But it's got that reputation for some annoying reason, which I would dearly love to have an opportunity to correct.

The Aldeburgh Festival in 1971 was, again, busy for Steuart. He was now, officially, the English Opera Group's Director of Music, and aside from playing in *King Arthur* and conducting a morning concert for the Society for Promotion of New Music featuring Pears in two new song-cycles, his main undertaking was *Noye's Fludde* in Orford Church, which was also to be televised.

◊

IT WAS ALL DONE with local people, which was very important to Ben. 'Local considerations matter to me most,' he said on one occasion – I think, when writing *A Midsummer Night's Dream*. 'Local considerations.' He was very anxious that his work should appeal, not just to cognoscenti but to local people, and that's why it's really written in that way; so that the young people of the schools from all over Suffolk could take part. It takes a virtuoso piece of organisation to make it happen. I think we had about seventy in the orchestra, crushed into Orford Church, and a large number of children as animals.

Ben was constantly around during rehearsals and enjoyed himself hugely. It's such a rewarding work to prepare. You start from virtually nothing, and slowly it grows, and the various disparate elements gradually come together. The final effect quite transcends its means. It was very difficult to keep a dry eye when the animals went into the ark singing 'Kyrie, eleison'. It's a very moving piece.

At the last, public, dress rehearsal there was an appalling moment. The audience is supposed to remain seated for the whole of the hymn 'Eternal Father, strong to save'. For some reason I signalled everyone to stand for the second verse, and as I did so, I caught sight of Ben, half on his feet, shaking his head in desperation, having just realised my error. But it was too late for me to reverse the process, so Ben and

Colin Graham made a great show of sitting down, as ostentatiously as possible, dragging the audience with them by sheer willpower.

Funnily enough he was never cross with me. He was always considerate and kind. If I got something wrong, he seemed to understand. I'm not quite sure why this was, because others didn't always have this experience. I can only assume that it was something to with the fact that I'm probably the only person of that set, working professionally with him, that he knew as a boy.

I tremble to think what my mother must have thought when I actually joined the English Opera Group, because her experiences were not always very happy. She must have suffered a lot over that, particularly as I got closer and closer as it were, and she thought I was going to be burned alive. So many people were. But I never felt that at any time, even if I really mucked it up. Because I have to say the performance of *The Beggar's Opera* that he came to – I thought I'd really had it. It was not good. For some reason we'd slipped a bit and during a syncopated bit everything came on the beat. It was terrible. I thought, 'He's not going to want to use me again.' But no, it didn't work that way. He was always very considerate and helpful.

◊

After the Festival, Steuart went to Drottningholm for more performances of *King Arthur* before the EOG's autumn season at Snape and Sadler's Wells, where he conducted *A Midsummer Night's Dream* for the first time and played in *The Turn of the Screw* under Britten's baton.

◊

I MANAGED TO TALK my way into playing the piano and celeste in the small, thirteen-part orchestra for the last time that Britten conducted *The Turn of the Screw*. It was a new production, again by Colin Graham, which opened in the Maltings before going to London. It was revived at the 1972 Aldeburgh Festival with Heather Harper as the Governess.

I practised it very, very carefully. There's quite a major piano part, with one scene which is virtually a concerto – the piano scene towards the end. So I was able, again, to watch him closely at work with his favourite players. And again I found the same strange thing: if he really had his favourite players, he let them have a little bit more freedom than he might have originally conceived. So all those cadenzas, for instance, in the opening of the second act, he didn't really conduct, he just let them play. I'm sure that he might have liked or wanted it to go slightly differently, but he never said anything.

Funnily enough, Ben wasn't as exacting as you might think. We all think of him as being fantastically exacting and one was made to think in those terms simply because here you are playing what is, after all, a masterpiece with its composer. What else can you do but respect what happens? This is the man who wrote this music, and he's capable of playing it himself on the piano to a wonderful standard, and giving you every sort of clue to how it goes. But when I went over the parts before recording it a few years later, an enormous number of mistakes reared up – silly things that shouldn't have been wrong. It was extraordinary that they had never really been properly checked.

On the first night, Ben took the piano scene so fast that I was hard pressed to keep up. We got to the scene – diddlydum, diddlydum, and all that – and I said to myself, 'This seems to be moving quite fast; I'd better watch out here.' And then it started to hot up, and by the time we got to the difficult stuff it was going like a bat out of hell. I thought I was going to fall off the piano stool.

Each performance was preceded by the luxury of a short orchestral rehearsal at which he would tidy up various points. He was particularly insistent that the harp and celeste flourishes at Fig. 17 in Act II should not last longer than a crochet. Starting the three long tremolando bars at Variation XV slowly and then making a gradual accelerando had already become part of the performing tradition. We were all surprised when a missing piano and timpani chord was reinstated after nearly twenty years. (Variation V, 4 bars before Fig. 48, should repeat the chord of the previous bar.)

I always used to talk to him after the performance about anything that needed attention, and a very interesting thing happened during the run. The end of the opera is surely one of the most overtly emotional passages that Britten ever wrote. It's the sort of thing Puccini might have even managed. (Dare I say it, dear Ben, don't turn in your grave!) But it is a Puccinian moment. When the Governess works herself up, it's a big moment. The truth is Ben was slightly embarrassed by that. When he was performing it, he tended to hurry on a little bit, not to give it any time or wallow in it. But there was one performance where he actually did give them more time, and he said to me afterwards, 'I gave the Governess a bit more time. I think it's better.' And I said, 'Yes, it is, much better. Wonderful.' But he didn't want to do that. His instinct told him that 'that's not the sort of music I write'. But there it is; you can't really get away from it, and I think you have to play it as a really big moment.

A lot of criticism comes his way that he wasn't able to write sensuous love music. This is disproved in many cases. I mean, you just have to think of Tytania in *A Midsummer Night's Dream* with Bottom, wonderfully sensuous music going on in the second act. And of course there's the Sid and Nancy stuff in *Albert Herring*. And actually there's a duet, 'Over the hills and far away' in *The Beggar's Opera*, that's realised with wonderful sensuality. It's a particularly beautiful number. That Second Lute Song in *Gloriana* knocks you out. It's so sensitive and sensual and has a real depth of emotion.

One of the challenges in *The Turn of the Screw* is the role of Miles. But it's brilliantly written for the boy. I mean, his notes are always given in the orchestra before he sings, it's never too complicated, and you don't realise when you listen to it that this is going on all the time. And it's always the girl that leads if there's anything dangerous, and provided the boy is reasonably accurate musically or reasonably competent musically, there is really no problem, and they often take to it like ducks to water. Provided the girl looks like a young girl and can actually do it musically, it is possible to have it sung by a young woman. I don't think the lullaby is very girly in the singing. Some of it is quite strong and not quite the sort of thing a young girl can manage. Although you could argue a lot with that, because it's a girl doing it. On the other hand, I think if he had a girl in mind he would have written it in a slightly different way.

That is the most wonderfully elliptical libretto, a wonderfully brilliant piece of work, because you never quite know what's going on at any time. All the way through you're always grasping for information. Will something be said that will actually tell you exactly what it is? It never happens. And that's what keeps you on tenterhooks right the way through. Myfanwy Piper does such a brilliant job with that, really brilliant. Every time I hear it, I think that Governess's narration will tell us the whole thing, but it doesn't. You don't know whether Miss Jessel is seen by Mrs Grose or whether she's making it up, and you don't know whether the ghosts are really there. You just don't know anything at all. And that's the undying fascination of the piece.

◊

London, 1999

I've been asked to understudy Aschenbach in *Death in Venice*, so who better to go to than the man himself, and see if he'll run through it with me. Yes, of course he will. When I arrive at Steuart's house in Highgate where he is in a state of mild excitement because a new washing machine is being delivered that day.

We run through the entire opera, with me feeling very nervous because of his history with the piece and him cheerfully singing in all the other roles. He points out various pitfalls. 'Just watch out here. This is where Peter always went wrong.' That sort of thing. Two hours later his washing machine arrives and I make for the front door, much the wiser.

'Now, I know this is awkward, but what do I owe you?' A double session like this from a professional coach would normally set me back fifty pounds or so.

'Don't be ridiculous.'

So I buy him a nice book when I get home, and he sends me a thank-you note saying I really needn't have.

The music profession is littered with singers and conductors who have been through Britten scores with Steuart. The soprano Mary Plazas was at Covent Garden early in her career, waiting in a corridor to do an audition, fretting because there was no sign of her pianist. Steuart was on his way to meet his wife Celia for lunch – she was working as a company manager for the Royal Opera at the time – and seeing Mary in the corridor, gave her a cheery hello.

'What are you doing here?'

'An audition, but there's no sign of my pianist!'

'Well, that won't do. Don't worry, I'll play for you.'

And so he did.

ELEVEN

O voluptuous days, O the joy I suffer

While Steuart was playing in the pit for Britten in *The Turn of the Screw*, he was conducting the other production in the English Opera Group season, *A Midsummer Night's Dream*. After the autumn run at Sadler's Wells, the *Dream* moved on to San Francisco, and Steuart made his US debut at the helm. Benjamin Luxon was singing Demetrius and in the new year of 1972, back in Britain, he and Steuart performed several recitals together.

Steuart conducted the new production for the English Opera Group that spring, John Gardner's *The Visitors*, which played in the Aldeburgh Festival. He was also back in the pit again for *The Turn of the Screw* and conducted some Stockhausen, which wasn't a popular choice for the festival-goers who rewarded it with boos.

Britten, meanwhile, was coming to the decision that he should stop conducting for a while, at least until he felt better and his ongoing heart issues were resolved. On 5 August, after the last performance of *The Turn of the Screw* in the 'Summer at the Maltings' season, Britten insisted on bringing the entire orchestra, including Steuart, on stage for a curtain call. It would turn out to be the last opera performance Britten ever conducted.

Since he was composing *Death in Venice* for performance the following year, this presented the issue of who would conduct it in his place. Although an announcement wasn't made until the following spring, it was clear there was only one candidate for the job. Steuart was of a different opinion.

◊

IT'S A QUESTION I often ask myself. Of all the people he could have chosen, why me?

I can't remember exactly what happened, but the invitation to conduct *Death in Venice* must have come after an English Opera Group meeting in which Colin Graham would have been the big white chief.

As it happened, I saw him in the street after the meeting and he said, 'You're going to be asked to do *Death in Venice*.'

I didn't believe it. I said, 'Oh yeah, right, fine.' I didn't believe it at all.

Colin and I got on very well. We got quite close. He was definitely a champion of mine.

Ben had never felt there had been a decent production of *A Midsummer Night's Dream* until Colin did his in 1967, and that was the one. I think because I got on so well with Colin, and he was very much the chosen one for directing Ben's operas, that was another thing in my favour.

Also I think it was important to get on with Peter Pears. You didn't want to make an enemy of him. I had no problem with that one. You could leave Peter to get on with it. He was very assiduous in getting things right. He was perfectly amenable as long as you observed the niceties. I think most people would say that Peter was very different when Ben wasn't around. He was much easier to deal with, much more at ease. He could be his own masterful self.

Anyway, despite my scepticism, I *was* asked to do *Death in Venice*, well before Ben was booked in for an operation. He told me he was planning to take over performances later on. He wanted to take a back seat, to watch what was going on, to advise, to correct anything that was wrong, without having the responsibility of conducting the performances. The fact that he eventually had to undergo major heart surgery has given rise to the misunderstanding that I was substituting for Ben at the premiere, but this wasn't the case. I was, of course, more thrilled than I can say at the prospect of my first Britten premiere.

◊

There turns out to be in *Death in Venice* a short but highly important counter-tenor part, and as when I write for the c-tenor I hear the voice of J. Bowman, I wonder if there's the slightest chance of you being a) interested b) inclined c) free or available – I don't suppose there is, because I know you are always so busy – and it *is* a short part: the Voice of Apollo, appearing in two crucial spots in the opera (the rehearsal time would therefore be very short for you). It would be marvellous to hear you in this my favourite of my operas (so far!) – but I don't really expect you to be able to do it, and if (sadly) not – whom could you recommend – a strong clear voice, up to top D?? Festival performances – 16–30 June, and then all September (Edinburgh, Maltings again, Venice, Flanders – Covent Garden in October (?)).

There was no mention of who would conduct, but Bowman didn't give it much thought.

I wasn't surprised when it turned out to be Steuart because I knew Ben implicitly trusted him enormously. He's a wonderful musician and was the obvious person to do it. I don't think anyone else was in the frame. [Charles] Mackerras possibly? I don't know. Steuart deserved to do it; he was the heir-apparent.

That Steuart was the heir-apparent would become more evident when, in November, Britten pulled out of a Decca recording of Percy Grainger's music at the eleventh hour, and Steuart was booked to replace him.

In November 1972 I was called in at relatively short notice to conduct Ben's second *Salute to Percy Grainger*, which Decca was to record at the Maltings. Ben's doctors were now forbidding him to conduct, but he was present at all the sessions, in the little control room, actually being much more positive than he was about any of his own music, strangely enough, and we enjoyed doing that enormously.

Ben and Peter both found Percy Grainger a fascinating personality, and they admired enormously the variety and the imagination of his arrangements. They were always putting them in programmes. 'Up She Goes', a concert we did in the 1968 Festival, had a lot of Grainger in it. Ben and Peter were very friendly with Stewart Manville, who was the Secretary of the Grainger Society, and who eventually married Ella, Grainger's widow, when he was forty-five and she eighty-three. I found him a very sinister character – something very odd about him.

The recording contains some memorable items, such as 'Under a Bridge', John Shirley-Quirk singing 'Dollar and a Half a Day', and Peter Pears singing 'The Three Ravens' and 'Brigg Fair'. In the original scheme of things, the final session was booked for Ben to record Mozart's early G minor Symphony (K183). It was clearly not appropriate for me to record Mozart for Ben, so what Grainger could we do with two oboes, two bassoons, four horns, and strings? I think it was Peter who suggested we try to make an instant arrangement of the 'Irish Tune from County Derry', of which he had innumerable chorus parts. We spent a fascinating evening working out the orchestration and marking in the instrumental cues (the players played from these chorus parts), and Ben was not at all hopeful that it would work. As it turned out, it did. Whether Percy Grainger would have approved we cannot tell, but he would surely have appreciated our application of his principles of elastic scoring.

For the next months, Steuart's chief focus would be on *Death in Venice*.

The score was gradually coming out, as they did in those days. Bit by bit, one got more sections of it – dyeline pages [a forerunner of photocopying] of the vocal score would arrive in the post. And I gradually got acquainted with it.

In December 1972, Rosamund Strode, Britten's music assistant, wrote to Steuart on Britten's behalf. As with *Owen Wingrave*, Myfanwy Piper was again the librettist and John Piper the designer.

Ben has asked me to let you know that there will be great *Death in Venice* discussions, etc., with the Pipers this coming weekend, and that he will probably be playing it through on Sunday [31 December]. I gather that we are letting you know of all such occasions!

It is quite likely that you could not possibly come, but perhaps you would like to give us a ring if there is any hope of you being here, to find out a bit more about the probable time involved. It is not likely to be late in the day as I understand the Pipers want to return home on Sunday.

◊

I HAD PERSUADED BEN, kept on at him. 'We must have a playthrough, let's do it.' He was very tired. He didn't want to do it. But of course, eventually we got two playthroughs; one of the first act – when I say the first act, up to the beginning of the Grecian games, the Games of Apollo – and then during the second he did the whole of the rest of it, all in one bang. They were in Halliford Street, their London home. I have very, very little memory of that first one. Except Ben playing the opening and saying, 'All these, not too long.'

The second one, I remember much more clearly, because I was turning the pages for him. Those occasions were really tense. When Ben was playing his music, particularly for the first time, he was extremely tense. You wouldn't believe how tense he could get. *Death in Venice* ends with this dance, high percussion right at the top of the piano. And then the tuba has to come in right at the bottom, boom, all at the same time as this stuff going on in the right hand . . . and he's doing all this, and I thought, 'Shall I put the tuba in for him, help him out a bit?' And I thought, 'No, I'll get it wrong.' I just froze. I thought, 'I can't do it.' And I just let him get on. He seemed to do it fine. It was terrific. We got to the end, he said, 'I played very badly', and rushed to the drinks cabinet.

The second playthrough, on 2 February, was the morning after an Aldeburgh gala concert in St James's Palace in the presence of The Queen Mother, who was Patron of the Aldeburgh Festival. The concert opened with Schubert's *Andantino varié* for piano duet – the only time I ever played four hands with Ben. We got off to a frightful start (it would be difficult to say which of us was more nervous), but we quickly settled down. Ben, who was playing the top part, was really in wonderful form. This must have been one of the last times that he played in public.

Ben could have been just a top-class pianist, but I suspect that some nervous tic would have taken over if playing the piano had been the only thing he did, because he was such a nervy person. It's very interesting how he was essentially an accompanist, that he was always aware of what else was going on. When he played for Peter there was absolutely no problem in ensemble because he was always with him entirely. But when we performed the Schubert, I was on the bottom part accompanying the top part, and we got off to the most horrendous start because he was following me and I was following him. It was very interesting, that dynamic. He didn't lead as I expected he would do, and I was trying to follow him and he was trying to follow me, for some reason. And so it all went to pieces with a terrible start. Peter said afterwards, 'Oh, it was Ben's fault entirely.' But it is interesting that he was the follower. He should have led really – it was his tune after all!

I seem to remember there was an announcement that night, at the gala concert, that I would be conducting *Death in Venice*. The play-through the next day was almost the last contact I had with Ben until well after the first night, over four months later.

When we were rehearsing in the Red House for the St James's Palace concert, I saw on Ben's desk his score of *Death in Venice*, so I could see he was getting on with the orchestration and they had got to the river-boat scene. Apparently, he had shown the score to Dmitri Shostakovich when he was visiting, and Shostakovich had taken the score away to peruse for a couple of hours. Ben was terribly nervous. Eventually Shostakovich reappeared and just said, 'Too many pauses.'

As the score was appearing there were also endless, *endless* corrections being sent out by Rosamund Strode, and there was one time when Ben rang me up to ask me how I'd like to have a certain page of bars numbered. Then there was the frightful moment when they discovered that the tune that Ben had set for the Strolling Players was in fact a popular song and still in copyright, and he had to rewrite the whole thing. That was a low moment. It was Myfanwy Piper who had found the tune on a trip to Venice, and she had just assumed it was old and out of copyright.

◊

Just as Steuart was getting into his preparations for *Death in Venice*, there was an unexpected turn of events. He was booked to conduct *Owen Wingrave* at Covent Garden the following month.

◊

WINGRAVE WAS DUE TO BE conducted by Gennady Rozhdestvensky but for some reason, having spent six weeks in draughty Russian corridors trying to get him free, Victor Hochhauser, the artists' agent and impresario, or whoever it was, could achieve nothing and gave up. So I stepped in, relatively late in the day.

I thought I'd better have a bit of a break before being plunged into these two big operas, so I decided to go away with the full score of *Death in Venice* and mark it. I spent a week in March in Switzerland; just me, in a room, with the score, listening to the whole thing in my head. If it was a nice day I'd ski, and if it was a bad day I'd stay in. It was a good way of doing it!

Sadly, there was an amazing number of errors, which Ben never normally used to make. All his scores used to be meticulous – you can never find a mistake in them, or only very occasionally. But here there was page after page of errors. So, clearly the onset of this illness was really affecting him and he was really struggling to get it finished. But he did, and I corrected the whole thing with what I hoped were corrections.

And then I visited Ben as he was, he said, 'being fattened for the kill' in the London Clinic, where he was sort of feeding up so he could be as strong as possible for the big operation. We went over various things, and there was a bit over a page that he'd left out completely, which he wrote into the score. There were lots of things we talked about. And that was almost the last time I saw him before the premiere.

We were rehearsing *Death in Venice* in the Donmar Warehouse at the same time as *Owen Wingrave* was opening at Covent Garden. It was a very complicated schedule but we managed all right. We had five weeks in all to get it on. These days they seem to need five years to compose an opera and another five years to rehearse it.

Of course, *Owen Wingrave* was also my debut with the Royal Opera House Orchestra. I was certainly nervous, but I think I was able to handle it. There were one or two crusty old players who had been around for years, a century it seemed, and I was only thirty-three at the time.

Here I was, making my Covent Garden debut with the world premiere of *Death in Venice* hot on its heels, but I wasn't aware that people were treating me any differently. I wasn't at all aware that I might have become a hot property, so to speak. I certainly didn't tout myself about with 'references'. I didn't go in for all that sort of thing. I just got my head down and got on with the job, and there was a lot of job to get on with.

◊

Pears was, of course, singing Aschenbach. It would be his last major role and a mammoth undertaking; Aschenbach never leaves the stage. James Bowman recalls that 'Peter knew Ben was dying. It was obvious. The whole thing was tinged with sadness. It was the music, it was Venice, it was the whole story, everybody knew it was the end of the road.'

I'm not so sure about that. When Ben went in for surgery, Peter came into rehearsal and just said, 'Ben's on the table', and got on with it as if nothing untoward was happening.

Myfanwy Piper was around a lot in rehearsals, but I don't think she changed many words, if any. Peter wanted the line 'my art is bent' changed, suspecting it would raise a giggle, but the subject matter and whether Ben himself was the subject of the piece never came up at all. We simply didn't have those sorts of conversations. It was never a big issue, not at all. We just got on and staged it.

Besides, this whole idea that opera is promoting homosexuality and all that, it's not really about that at all. One of the lines of recitative Ben tried to cut has Aschenbach saying, 'Yes, I have grown reserved, self-sufficient, since the death of a wife and the marriage of an only daughter.' He wanted to cut the line and I persuaded him to put it back. He said, 'We only put it in as a sop for the people that think Aschenbach was a poof.' But I thought it was important that the line should be there for precisely that reason. He was a married man and he had children. It wasn't about homosexual love at all. It was about the very concept of beauty and detachment and all the Dionysiac urges which we all have.

A page from Steuart Bedford's conducting score of *Death in Venice*, showing the reinstated passage of recitative

No one apart from Pears was quite prepared for how absent Britten would be from the process of mounting the opera. 'Ben didn't have much of a hand in it at all,' according to James Bowman. 'It's all a myth that Steuart would go and see Ben every evening. He hardly ever saw him.'

It's a myth that might have sprung from an article in *The Times*, timed to coincide with the opera's premiere in June, in which Steuart was quoted as saying, 'We've been right through the score and talked a great deal about it.'

◊

I CAN'T HAVE SAID THAT, simply because it wasn't true! I suspect it came from the publicity department. There was, in fact, one bedside consultation in the Red House during the production period. And that was about a cut that Colin Graham desperately wanted to do, the interlude between Figs. 115 and 117 in Act I, the gondola music. Ben saw the point immediately and agreed to the cut, but the passage found its way back in the revisions of the following year, with a new vocal line added for Aschenbach. But that was the only time Ben had any input into the staging, or the musical side of the performance.

One day, I had the percussion section alone and we got to the nightmare scene, way into the second act. We were doing quite well,

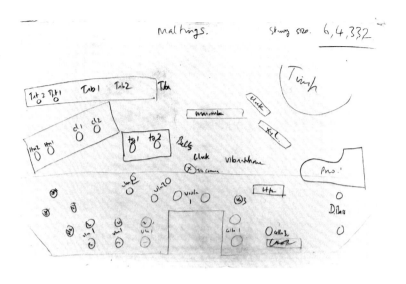

Covent Garden

Orchestral layout for *Death in Venice*, Snape (above) and Covent Garden (below), drawn by Steuart Bedford in the back pages of his conducting score.

and there's a bit where there are eight bars all the same – *baw, baw, baw, baw* – just going on like that, and I was thinking while we were doing it that I should just cut on . . . I wasn't really thinking, just beating away and turning the manuscript to have a look at where to cut on to . . . And we got to the explosion bit and I nearly died. I jumped out of my skin. I wasn't ready for it. It made such a noise.

Frederick Ashton, who was choreographing the dance elements of the opera, wasn't too wild about the piece. There was a lot of discussion about cuts he wanted to make, because the Pentathlon scene is just a little bit too long, the two numbers just before it starts. Ben came up with some cuts, which I've always done since.

There were no occasions I can recall when we thought, 'Oh, I wish the composer was here to sort this out!' And whereas the composer might normally sit in the auditorium for the stage rehearsals, to give notes on the piece as a whole, of course we didn't have that. We just had the music staff, and because Peter was on stage all the time, he couldn't sit and watch and act as Ben's eyes and ears.

As we progressed, I still really wanted Ben to hear the piece, so I came to an agreement with the orchestra that we should record the stage and orchestra rehearsals. I listened to the tapes, but Ben never really wanted to. He decided not to.

Still, I think we were aware at the premiere that there was still work to be done on it, in terms of cuts and such. It was still 'work in progress' as far as we were concerned.

The day before the premiere, Ben left Aldeburgh for Horham and stayed there for most of the Festival. Here was this major premiere and its composer was a few miles away on the Norfolk border. He hadn't heard a note of it.

In the audience on the first night were Steuart's parents, the 'Leslieys'. So too was *Opera* magazine's critic, Alan Blyth, who described Steuart's conducting as 'masterly'.

Above Death in Venice, Snape Maltings, 1973:
Robert Huguenin (Tadzio) and Peter Pears (Aschenbach).
Below Pears, Colin Graham and Steuart Bedford in the Piazza San Marco, Venice,
during rehearsals for *Death in Venice* at La Fenice, 1973.

Rehearsals for *Phaedra*, Aldeburgh Festival 1976:
above Janet Baker, Benjamin Britten and Steuart Bedford;
below orchestral rehearsal with the English Chamber Orchestra
in Thorpeness Working Men's Club; with Britten are Rita Thomson,
Colin Matthews and Rosamund Strode.

Rehearsal for *Canticle IV: 'The Journey of the Magi'*, Festival of Flanders, 1974;
Steuart Bedford with James Bowman, Peter Pears and John Shirley-Quirk.

Backstage at Snape Maltings, 1977: Janet Baker, Steuart Bedford and
John Shirley-Quirk before a performance of Wolf's *Italienisches Liederbuch*.

Steuart Bedford and the English Chamber Orchestra at Snape Maltings, 1982:
above with Isaac Stern and Mstislav Rostropovich rehearsing Brahms's
Double Concerto; *below* timpanist David Corkhill reads a newspaper.
(The lower photograph is displayed in the Bedford lavatory.)

Death in Venice wasn't Steuart's only commitment at the 1973 Aldeburgh Festival. He played in a chamber concert, and directed the English Chamber Orchestra and Geraint Evans in an evening of Mozart, Haydn and Cimarosa. He was also appointed as an Artistic Director of the Festival for the forthcoming years.

Shortly after the Festival, Steuart was driving to King's Lynn to play the piano in a performance of Britten's Canticles, featuring the three principal singers from *Death in Venice*: Peter Pears, John Shirley-Quirk and James Bowman.

Peter had a fine sense of humour – which you wouldn't have expected. I can remember a rehearsal of *'The Journey of the Magi'* [Canticle IV] with Quirky and James, and I've never laughed so much in my life. There was something so funny about them trying to get it right. James was joshing Pears on the stomach, Quirky was being very, very serious. It was a strange thing, these three great singers standing together, and every time there was a rest they would all puff out a sigh as if to say, 'Was that right?'

The ride in the car to King's Lynn was hilarious. Peter asked James if he had any magazines.

'Magazines?' said James, coyly. 'What – *Vogue*, *Exchange & Mart*?'

'No. Magazines. You know. Magazines.'

'Oh, magazines!'

And James, rather than send him some – can you imagine the look on the face of Rita Thomson, Britten's nurse, if she opened the package by mistake? – slipped a brown envelope under Peter's dressing-room door one night.

◊

THE SECOND PERFORMANCE of *Death in Venice* at the Maltings was a live broadcast, and I hoped Ben would listen to it then. Well, he turned on the radio, and the minute the opera started he heard a strange buzzing sound. He didn't know what it was at all – he thought something had gone wrong with his radio and turned it off. He had heard practically none of it at all. The sound he heard, the buzzing which the BBC microphones had picked up, was the motors of the periaktoi, the revolving pillars, which were part of the production. The loud hum of that completely distracted him. He didn't know what it was. He thought something had gone wrong. So that was that.

We had scheduled a special performance of *Death in Venice* for him, in the summer season at the Maltings; a sort of semi-private performance, especially for the composer, in September, so he could have a few months to recover from his very serious operation. Let's not forget he'd also had a stroke coming around from the anaesthetic, which had partly paralysed his right side, leaving him very much more frail than he would normally have been. Now, given the way he tended to react to his own music, I felt that to plaster him in front of the whole piece, which he'd never seen or heard, would be quite a strain. So I thought the only thing I could do was to take a tape of the BBC broadcast down to the Red House and play it to him there; just play it to him so he hears the music, so he's not presented with the whole thing in one tremendous bang.

Here was a really a major opera – a major work of a very, very major composer – and here was I, driving down to the Red House to play him this piece which he'd never heard. I can't think anybody has ever been in a similar situation. Can you imagine going down to Wahnfried, playing *Parsifal* to Wagner because he was too ill to hear it? It was quite a nerve-racking experience. And I wasn't quite sure which of us was more nervous, him or me.

As he listened, he said very little. He did not like the Apollo and Hyacinthus chorus – his part of it, not ours – and he found 'The players are here' chorus somewhat too fast. The only other person there was Peter, who endeavoured to lighten the situation a little bit, as he came across one of his notorious word changes – in the pursuit scene there was a bit he could never get right – and he said, 'Oh, Steuart is crawling out of the pit to get me on track here.' Ben listened very seriously and intently, right the way through. And at the end, he simply said, 'Is it all right?' I didn't really know what to say. It was quite alarming, and I'm sure I said, 'It's magnificent. It's wonderful. It's a great work.'

And I'm sure Peter agreed too, at which point we reached again for the drinks cabinet.

The Other Bedfords

In the narrative of Steuart's life with Britten, some of the leading characters from his early life have disappeared. The Two Leslieys come regularly to Steuart's performances, but Lesley never draws comparisons between, say, Steuart's reading of *The Rape of Lucretia* and the performances she sang herself under Britten's baton. Leslie, other-worldly and quietly genial, never complains that he misses the friendship of Ben and Peter, nor – as far as we know – does he quiz his wife as to why she and her once close friends now seem a little distant. If she has qualms about Steuart being in the Aldeburgh circle, no doubt her pride at her son's achievements far outweigh any personal misgivings.

Steuart's oldest brother Peter sings in the ensemble of the Church Parables but his singing career is not flourishing.

David's career has taken, and continues to take, some interesting turns that see him flit in and out of the Aldeburgh fold. His studies with Nono in Milan have earned him the label of 'avant-garde composer', but from the late 1960s he becomes fascinated with rock music, and in 1969 joins Mike Oldfield in the psychedelic rock band Kevin Ayers and the Whole World, which tours in 1970 and records an album. David also orchestrates Oldfield's hugely successful *Tubular Bells*, and Steuart plays the organ on the recording. But in the midst of David's rock career – a genre completely alien to both Britten and Steuart – David is commissioned twice by Peter Pears to write song-cycles for tenor and small ensemble – *The Tentacles of the Dark Nebula* (with a text by the science-fiction writer Arthur C. Clarke) and *When I Heard the Learn'd Astronomer* (Walt Whitman) – both of which are performed at the Aldeburgh Festival. In 1977, Pears commissions David again; a short cycle of more Whitman poems, for two tenors (Pears and Ian Partridge), piano and small organ, *On the Beach at Night*. At its premiere at the 1978 Festival, Steuart plays the piano.

Steuart Bedford with his brother David, Snape Maltings, June 1978.

TWELVE

So the moments pass

On the 12 September 1973, Ben saw *Death in Venice* for the first time. He sat in the middle of the auditorium, in a wheelchair. There were various other friends there too. He didn't give me any notes, but we must have had a discussion at some point. He was delighted with Colin Graham's and Frederick Ashton's work, but as to his own contribution, Ben was not satisfied.

After its premiere at the Maltings, *Death in Venice* went that year to Edinburgh, back to Snape, Venice, Brussels and Covent Garden.

Curiously enough, Venice was having a typhoid epidemic at the time, and we all had to be inoculated for cholera.

For the Covent Garden performances in October Ben undertook a large number of revisions, particularly in the Games of Apollo section, where many of the gaps were shortened and a striking timpani ostinato added. In several places he wanted more orchestral colour, such as the two piccolos and oboe in Aschenbach's 'Mysterious Gondola' and the suspended cymbal in the Overture. Further revisions followed, to be incorporated into the Decca recording the following spring. Even this was not the end: in October, on the morning of our final dress rehearsal in New York, there arrived a new version of the end of the hotel guests' scene in Act I. Had it arrived two hours later, it would have been too late.

A page from Steuart Bedford's conducting score of *Death in Venice*.

Pears was having constant problems remembering Aschenbach's words. In a tribute book to celebrate Pears's seventy-fifth birthday, Steuart wrote:

'Should I give up the fruitless struggle with the word?' Thus exclaims Aschenbach near the start of the opera *Death in Venice*. I do not think I am betraying any professional secrets when I say that Peter would have been only too happy to answer this question in the affirmative not from any drying up or inspiration, which was Aschenbach's trouble, but simply because of his own particular difficulty in remembering that word.

With Peter this problem would usually manifest itself with his forgetting not the whole sentence but just one or two constituent words; the noun, adjective or verb. That he was almost always ready with a more than satisfactory alternative is just one, albeit a small one, of the fascinating sidelines of his art to which I would like to pay tribute.

Peter very rarely dried up totally on stage, though he did have a blank spot about Nebuchadnezzar's opening line in *The Burning Fiery Furnace*, 'Adept in magic', which was probably due to the unlikely nature of the line and its apparent illogicality. Also sheer nonsense was very rare, 'Back Collatinus!' in *The Rape of Lucretia* being the exception that proves the rule. When a line did escape him altogether, and he was reduced to singing what he himself referred to as 'verbal chewing-gum', he somehow managed, by stage presence and force of personality, to convince the audience that their puzzled incomprehension was due entirely to a lack of concentration on their part.

Occasionally he would start a word and then suddenly realise that he should be singing another, changing in mid-stream with interesting results. For example, he once started the word 'fate' and realised before reaching the letter 't' that he should have been singing the word 'case'. So what the audience heard was 'desperate indeed is his face'.

However, it is the spontaneous invention of new words to suit the emergency that turns this weakness into an amazing source of strength, making his struggle with the word far from fruitless. Often the alternative became the preferred version and was taken over by the librettist. *Death in Venice* positively teems with examples, but the process was well established by the time of the first of the Church Operas, *Curlew River.* 'It ill becomes you, Curlew Ferryman, such incivility,' sings the Madwoman. But Peter would invariably produce 'It ill befits . . .' showing an unconscious preference for a double 'f' alliteration rather than the hard double 'c': then, not always being certain of what it was that ill befitted the Ferryman, he would sometimes substitute 'importunity'. One only needs to call upon poetic licence to defend this.

In over thirty-five performances (and the attendant rehearsals) that I must have conducted with Peter of *Death in Venice,* the wealth of spontaneous creativity that he exhibited could almost have a volume to itself. To illustrate the process I would ask the reader to imagine himself faced with the sentence '. . . but the truth is that it has been precipitated by a sudden desire for the unknown' and further to imagine that he has forgotten the word 'precipitated'. How many of us could without hesitation read the line substituting an alternative five-syllable word? In two successive performances Peter first gave 'accelerated' and then at the next performance found a second alternative, 'initiated', both without the slightest hesitation.

Time and again an adjective would desert him and an immediate appropriate replacement be found – 'that absurd obstinate gondolier' became an 'absurd truculent gondolier' or 'so I had to mock myself as the crestfallen lover' became 'star-crossed lover'.

But the masterpiece has always seemed to me his version of the line 'the city fathers are rarely so serious'. Coming to the line at a comparatively late rehearsal for the premiere, Peter suddenly substituted 'seldom' for 'rarely', which with 'serious' makes a nice alliteration. However, having begun with 'seldom', he proceeded to trump his own ace with 'solicitous'. In the printed libretto the line now reads 'the city fathers are seldom so solicitous'.

In the tribute, Steuart omitted to mention one of Pears's other aberrations.

He was quite capable of something like this: 'So it has come to this. I can find no better description of my state than the hackneyed words . . .' And then he couldn't remember what the heck the words were, and so he had to turn upstage and mumble gobbledegook. He couldn't remember 'I love you'. That seems to be quite extraordinary, quite extraordinary.

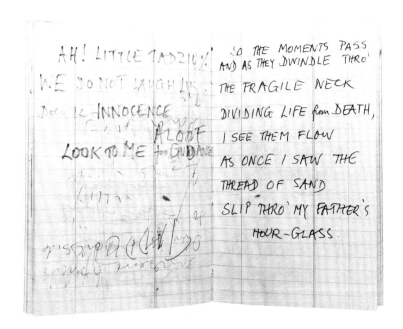

Peter Pears's prop notebook for *Death in Venice*.

Steuart's commitments to the English Opera Group were not confined to *Death in Venice*. In the second half of 1973, he also conducted *Idomeneo* and a double-bill of Tchaikovsky's *Iolanta* and Gilbert and Sullivan's *Trial by Jury*, and in December he conducted *The Turn of the Screw* for the first time, in Geneva, with Pears singing Quint. (During October he made the rare transition from conducting Britten at Covent Garden on Wednesday the 24th, to Gilbert and Sullivan at Sadler's Wells the next night, Thursday the 25th).

After conducting a production of *Idomeneo* for Welsh National Opera in March of 1974, Steuart returned to Snape in April to record *Death in Venice* for Decca.

When we recorded *Death in Venice* in 1974, Ben really did take a back seat and quietly sat in a dressing room listening, as they called it, on 'granny level', surrounded by Rita Thomson and Co., and given a whisky or a brandy every so often. Sometimes he couldn't cope any longer and went. Somebody wrote somewhere that he got over-excited during the recordings and over-exerted himself, but that's rubbish. That never happened. He took a back seat. And he said very little. He was very, very weak at the end of that. We were all very worried about him. That was virtually a dead year as far as he was concerned. That was the time when I persuaded him to see Margaret Sampson, who had helped me with depression.

We made a cut for the recording – an early recitative that seemed far too long – but when we returned to do it on stage we realised that we needed a long recitative to give John Shirley-Quirk enough time for his costume change, from the Traveller to the Elderly Fop, so we opened up the cut again to give him time. But it has caused confusion ever since, as people tend to think that the version on the recording is Ben's definitive version.

Sometime after that I can remember going down to Horham – I think I stayed the night – because he wanted to work on *Death in Venice*, to get the metronome marks in. We had an almost giggly session, the whole morning spent working out what we should do, and how we should define some of the stylistic features, whether we should write a note about how to play certain things. He was in a very good mood, unusually so that time, because usually he was very black and dark and serious. But that was a lighter occasion, very nice. Ben tried to get metronome markings in all the early pieces but he couldn't get them into all the parts. He would have needed a librarian to himself for a month, so he gave up on that one.

In his first year as an Artistic Director of the Aldeburgh Festival, Steuart conducted a Holst double-bill of *Sāvitri* and *The Wandering Scholar*, with a line-up that included Janet Baker, Philip Langridge, Robert Tear, John Shirley-Quirk and Norma Burrowes, and Purcell's *Dido and Aeneas*, again with Janet Baker. He also accompanied the 'Aldeburgh Quartet' – Heather Harper, Janet Baker, Peter Pears and John Shirley-Quirk – in a programme of Mozart, Schumann and Britten. This was the first time that numbers from *Paul Bunyan* had been heard in public since its disastrous premiere in New York in 1941.

We all knew that *Paul Bunyan* existed, but not many of us had ever seen a note of it. Keith Grant (the General Manager of the English Opera Group up to 1973) took over as General Secretary of the Royal Society of Arts, and he somehow persuaded Peter to give a lecture about *Paul Bunyan*, with musical examples. While we were recording *Death in Venice*, Peter gathered up a bunch of the chorus and said, 'Try this, we'll sing through these numbers.' And here we were seeing the Food Chorus, Christmas Party . . . a lot of numbers. And so we went along to illustrate Peter's talk, where he sang Inkslinger. None of us except Peter, who had copied out much of the score back in 1941, had the faintest notion of what it was like, so the freshness and vitality of the music came as a wonderful surprise. The lecture at the RSA was the first European hearing of any of the music.

The next thing we knew was that Ben decided to allow us to perform some of them as excerpts, with piano, at the upcoming Aldeburgh Festival. I'm not quite sure how that happened, but Peter must have lent on him a little bit saying, 'We must do these, they're so much fun.' This was a time when Ben was looking at his earlier pieces, and trying to work out if there was any mileage in just dressing them up and doing them. And several pieces did come out from that period, some early songs, piano pieces and others.

So we performed these numbers from *Paul Bunyan* at the Festival, with piano. The so-called 'Aldeburgh Quartet' relished being cats, cooks, lumberjacks, and a telegram boy. The day before the concert we sang the music all through for Ben at the Red House. It was quite evident that he had lost none of his acuity, drawing my attention to the *moderato* indication for the Western Union Boy, and steadying up the Cats' Duet, both of which I had been taking too fast.

Steuart conducted the Holst double-bill at the BBC Proms, *Dido* at the Cheltenham Festival, and later recorded them both.

◊

IN 1974 WE STAGED a new production of *Albert Herring* by David William – a rather splendid production, very beautifully done – with Anthony Rolfe Johnson in the lead and Thomas Allen as Sid. Pauline Tinsley did her first Lady Billows. A wonderful cast. As always with that piece we had a wonderful time. Ben came to one of the stage and orchestra rehearsals. I used to go back to the Red House afterwards and talk about things, and he said, when we had done the second act, that he'd like to have a session with me and Tony Rolfe Johnson, just to go over various points in the big post-party scene, Act II scene 2.

So we went up to the Red House and I suddenly got the impression that Ben was really trying to impart something that he wasn't going to be able to impart again. He went to extraordinary detail, mentioning

Top Murray Perahia, Steuart Bedford, John Shirley-Quirk, Heather Harper, Sarah Walker and Marie McLaughlin rehearsing for a gala concert marking Peter Pears's seventieth birthday on 22 June 1980.
Below Steuart Bedford with Marie McLaughlin (Tytania) backstage at Snape Maltings during a performance of *A Midsummer Night's Dream*, 7 June 1980.

At the reception after the Patron's Choice concert, 13 June 1975,
Benjamin Britten, Rita Thomas, Steuart Bedford and Lady Penn.

After an orchestral concert including 'Billy in the Darbies', 19 June 1975,
Steuart Bedford, his mother Lesley and Theodor (Ted) Uppman,
who created the role of Billy Budd.

Lennox Berkeley, Steuart Bedford, Peter Pears and Ian Partridge rehearsing for a concert that included the first performance of the revised version of Berkeley's *Four Ronsard Sonnets*, at the 1978 Aldeburgh Festival.

Steuart Bedford with Murray Perahia and John Ogdon, 1977 Aldeburgh Festival.

1979 Aldeburgh Festival: Steuart Bedford (*above*) with Jonathan Miller after Miller's lecture , 'The Opera in Question', and (*below*) with William and Susana Walton during rehearsals for the first complete performance of Walton's *Façade 2*.

all sorts of fascinating things. He had conducted innumerable performances of the piece and was most lucid about the problems.

I was intrigued by the way he conducted a section of Albert's Act II monologue, taking it in two from Figs. 92 to 93 and beyond. 'Bounce me high' was intended to move at a very steady tempo; it can so easily get faster and faster.

At the end of our session Ben handed me the manuscript full score – all three volumes – and said, 'Take this if you like; it's been on the road many times.' Quite aside from the responsibility of having such an important document in my possession, the thought of what Rosamund Strode, Ben's faithful and devoted archivist, would have said compelled me to decline the offer.

The minute I got back, I wrote down everything he'd said.

When Albert is drunk, all the tempos marked 'as before' need to be slightly steadier than before, as when one is inebriated the thought processes are slowed down. This also has the benefit of allowing Albert to stress each quaver on the words 'good' and 'reign'. Ben also wanted me to give Albert time through the section 'With enormous care'. And a very characteristic Britten thing: when Albert sings 'Pretty name, Nancy, pretty name', it goes onto a C sharp. Now that changes the harmony, and practically everyone slows down and underlines that change of harmony. But in fact, it's not written that way, and he drew our attention to this. 'No, don't make that long, make it very short. Just touch it. That is, don't overdo the change in harmony. Don't throw it at the audience that way, make them listen to it.' And that's a feature that you do find a lot. It's not overwritten or stressed.

The eventual resolution of the '*Tristan*' chord in an earlier recitative [where Britten references Wagner] is another example; the harmony is especially felicitous, and all one's instincts are to dwell on the chord for a little, but it is marked *pp* with a staccato dash. At the end of *The Turn of the Screw* we can see the same process on a larger scale.

In the final 'Malo' reprise the harmonies are heard once and once only and not for longer than a quaver.

Ben had many requests for the characterisation of Albert:

'It's your little Albert! You sugar-plum' – with great charm.
'Dark in here!' – whispered.
'But I'm blowed if I'm ready for that!' – suddenly strong.
'We've never talked or walked' – very bitter, lots of words.
'But when, but when . . .' – breaths in all the rests.
'The tide will turn' – really sung.
'I'll toss for it – and damn the risk!' – suddenly decisive.

There were all sorts of other things, especially about me not going too fast. It was a very, very fascinating session.

In a note to me written after the first night, Ben expressed the hope that I had 'enjoyed working on the old piece'.

◊

At the end of September 1974, Steuart found himself on his way to the Metropolitan Opera, New York, to conduct the American premiere of *Death in Venice* with Pears and Shirley-Quirk resuming their roles. He arrived on the 28th, with the opening night just three weeks away.

I was a late-ish replacement for someone else. I'm not possessive about *Death in Venice*. Not really. I don't see why other people shouldn't be allowed to conduct it.

On 3 October, Pears wrote to Britten:

Everything here is as you might expect, but I think D in V should go on OK. Steuart is pleased with the Orchestra, though I think the percussion Dept. was slightly dazed!

Meanwhile, Britten was writing to Pears. Donald Mitchell had heard the German premiere and relayed some thoughts to Britten.

> He had one or two *good* pts. to make, & I'll be writing to Stewy about one suggested alteration (Hotel Guests).

Clearly, in private, Steuart was still referred to occasionally by his childhood name. The alteration arrived just in time for the dress rehearsal.

On the 12th, Pears wrote again to Britten, reporting on the progress of rehearsals and mourning the absence of the original Tadzio, the object of Aschenbach's obsession. Robert Huguenin's Tadzio had appeared to be on the cusp between innocence and knowingness. Pears had liked the young dancer, was attracted to him both in and out of character, and had much enjoyed working with him in the first production.

> Things are going alright here, I think – up & down & the stage-lighting rehearsals are always a bit tiring. Stop – Stop – Stop & start & wait & stop, etc., etc. But Steuart is doing v well with the orchestra which is good and happy. Percussion getting better every day, really rhythmic and sure, and the bigger number of strings *is* better, sounds so much richer. [. . .] I miss Bob Huguenin *very* much. This boy Bryan [Pitts] is a much better dancer; he is from Balanchine's Co. & as light as air, very fine movements, & the new dance is v. elegant and fine. But he has *not got IT* at all!! Oh dear! I *wouldn't* dream of looking at him for more than 5 seconds. A sweet chap and all that, 19 or 20 years old, blond from N. Carolina, but no Bob. I have written to Bob to tell him so, it might cheer him up a bit!

The opera was a big success in New York, and Steuart was invited to return the following season to conduct *Le nozze di Figaro*. Pears was being less than honest with Britten in his letter.

I'm afraid it's true that Peter had various relationships with somewhat disreputable men. Colin Graham said that he had a major obsession with Bob Huguenin, our first Tadzio. It's fatal of course to have a boy like that anywhere near Peter. In New York he had quite a bingo with the dancer who played Tadzio, but I don't know how far it went. Obviously, I had to turn a blind eye to Peter's indiscretions. It does raise the question again of Peter's 'power' over Ben. Thomas Hemsley certainly believed that Ben was always so afraid that Peter would leave him, that it gave Peter too much control.

Meanwhile, performances of *Albert Herring* were still in the EOG calendar, and Steuart dutifully flew back from New York to conduct *Herring* in Leeds and Newcastle. The next season, when conducting the Met's *Figaro* on tour – in Atlanta, Dallas, Minneapolis and Detroit – he would fly back to Britain between each performance to conduct the EOG's *Iolanta/Trial by Jury* double-bill on tour at home.

While we were in New York, I sent him a card. He was always punctilious if you sent him a postcard; he always replied. However busy he might be, he always seemed to have time to reply, which was so good. And he said to me on a card, 'I've just written a new piece, which I'm dying to show to you, for next year.' This was the *Suite on English Folk Tunes, 'A time there was . . .'*. So I got to see that and when we went over it he said, as he always did about *The Beggar's Opera* too, 'Such lovely tunes!' Always the tunes.

On 23 November, Steuart wrote to Britten from New York:

I seem to be incapable of remembering birthdays and it was only when I heard an all-BB programme put out by one of the more civilised radio stations that I finally 'twigged'. By the time this arrives no doubt the cake will be finished but nonetheless all good wishes retrospective and otherwise and I trust that you are still in good spirits.

Peter was on marvellous form again last Tuesday in another very good and enthusiastically received performance. However my first night favourite 'inextangible longing' was almost superseded by 'just as I indulge myself in these novelist's scoplications'.

Last night I was invited (through the Met. vibraphone player, whose wife was to play the harp) to a performance of 'the Screw' put on by the 'Eastern Opera Theater', a fringe company using young professionals rather like London's Opera da Camera. In many ways it was a very creditable show with an excellent orchestra and very well sung Governess. Unfortunately the theatre was a disaster – no pit but so wide that players could easily squeeze into a corner without obscuring the stage. They played at stalls level on a carpet so the sound was totally dead – but the music still triumphed and it was much appreciated.

I can't wait to see the new piece!

As soon as he got Steuart's letter, Britten wrote straight back.

It was lovely to get your letter with first-hand news of musical life in New York. It is marvellous that Peter continues in such wonderful form and I am delighted that his literary invention is as rich as ever. I quite frequently telephone to him and he never fails to thank God for your cooperation 'in the pit'.

I long to show you the new piece and Rosamund and I have just about completed the full score. Perhaps when you are back from New York a little visit to Aldeburgh might be possible to arrange. I have a sneaking feeling that it might be rather good; certainly the tunes are marvellous.

The spring of 1975 saw the next stage in reviving *Paul Bunyan*. The English Opera Group was being wound up, to be replaced by English Music Theatre, with Colin Graham as its Artistic Director.

◊

COLIN WANTED SOMETHING spectacular with which to launch English Music Theatre. Ben had always been very ticklish about what people thought about his music, and because the New York premiere of *Paul Bunyan* in 1941 had been a disaster, Ben had withdrawn the piece completely. Nobody was allowed to do it, to see it, until Colin got a bee in his bonnet, determined to get this premiere into the first season in 1976.

The first thing was to get Ben to look at it again, which he was very reluctant to do. After lots of pushing, eventually Ben relented, but he said there were conditions. First, we had to do a concert performance, which the BBC could take, with actors, so he could get a complete idea of how the piece sounded. Second, he had the sole right to cut or rewrite numbers. That was quite a big job. Colin Matthews [the composer, who was working with Britten as a music assistant], I think, had the biggest work to do with that.

So we did a concert performance for the BBC in Manchester. George Hamilton IV, the American Country & Western singer, was booked to do the Narrator. At our first rehearsal I couldn't hear him at all. All that came out was this very faint, mumbly croon. And I thought, 'Jesus Christ, this is going to be a disaster!' But when he got a microphone and amplification he was fine.

It was that BBC performance that finally persuaded Ben. He'd been very reluctant to let it out, largely due to the appalling trauma of the first performance, which had been so roundly pounced on by the critics, particularly the rather acidulous Virgil Thomson. He'd really put it back in the cupboard and not really wanted to have anything to do with it. All the trauma of that came back to him.

When he finally allowed it out, he was still not easy about it, and he undertook several revisions, which I now begin to feel were based on panic rather than on mature reflection. And he was capable of panic, we have to remember. The last act of *A Midsummer Night's Dream*, for instance, contains a section that was cut at the first performance. And he said once about that, 'Yes, I know, we did cut it. It was because by the time we'd rehearsed the first two acts and we were into the third act, we all panicked. And I had felt I had to shorten it. I thought it was going to be too long.' And so they did. You could probably imagine what it must be like rehearsing *A Midsummer Night's Dream* for the very, very first time. I mean, it must have taken ages to do it – it's a very difficult piece. And so you can well imagine by Act III they were beginning to panic. But in fact that cut, if you make it, means that the lovers wake up alarmingly quickly. They go from sleep to fully awake in a very, very short time. And I did persuade him when I did it in 1971 to let me open it up, which therefore would mean it was the first time it had ever been heard. And I've never ever done it without. Well, I have done it without, but only under the greatest protest. But whenever I do it, I always try to keep it in. It works beautifully, with lots of offstage horns. And when we finally heard it, when I did it as Sadler's Wells, he said, 'Oh yes, I quite like that new bit.' He really liked it and he was happy with that.

I feel the same about some of the changes he made in *Paul Bunyan*, particularly with the shortening of Slim's aria, which was sort of over before it had begun. And one or two things that we did change along the way, at rehearsals when he was there. But we knew he was still petrified about the whole thing, because when it came to the performances in 1976, he wouldn't go into his box at all, but sat on the steps outside, no doubt biting his nails.

I've been quite cavalier about restoring some of the cuts he made, particularly Slim's aria, at the end of the first act. Ben had taken out about three-quarters of it – and the song then became a nothing.

Whereas it's a big number, and rather wonderful if you do it uncut, which I always do now. There are bits I would love to re-examine, to see if they would work. The 'Lullaby of Dream Shadows' for instance, which is included on the recording made by Philip Brunelle, but otherwise has been rarely heard. It is very long, but it should possibly go in the second act, rather than the first, which is already rather long. But then, would it work with the text? The Prologue too is very curious. I've not quite been able to work it out yet.

I'm not sure how much influence Peter had on the cuts. We know that Peter influenced the major revision of *Billy Budd*, largely because Peter hated singing the big Muster scene, naughtily known as the 'I am the captain of the Pinafore' scene. He found it very difficult. But the reasons for cutting *Paul Bunyan* and *Billy Budd* are very different. And we shouldn't think that Ben's final version of *Paul Bunyan* is necessarily the best version.

People tend to blame W. H. Auden, who wrote the libretto, for *Paul Bunyan*'s lack of success to date. It is true that he made no allowance for how a long-spun vocal line would affect the comprehensibility of his words, and that the subject matter is rather fantastic for the present day and age. And it's interesting that Leonard Bernstein struggled with writing a European musical, *Candide*, while Britten struggled with writing an American one.

Britten never heard the original, full version of *Paul Bunyan* after its first run. No one would dare play that old version, not even me. But if I'd had more time with Ben I think I could have persuaded him to open lots of the cuts. I'm sure I could.

Aldeburgh, August 2020

Steuart has just read the second draft of this book. I didn't let him read the first draft because it needed some outside eyes to look at it first. Besides, I was too terrified he would pooh-pooh the whole thing, not necessarily from the point of view of Steuart the conductor and friend of Britten, but from the standpoint of a Parkinson's sufferer and a son with an eye to his mother's dignity and reputation.

Something else has happened too which has left him fragile and distracted, and working on his memoir is not at the top of his priorities.

On Easter Day, Steuart called me at home. We exchanged some of the usual chat. Happy Easter. The pandemic. His health. The weather.

Then he said, 'Look, I'm afraid I've got some rather disastrous news. Celia died yesterday.'

Celia had been diagnosed with cancer of the liver in February, and while I knew she was very ill, this was still a terrible shock.

'What am I going to do now?' he said.

It's a question I couldn't answer.

This wasn't the plan. The plan was that strong Celia, endlessly patient and kind Celia, was going to manage Steuart's care and navigate the murky waters of his decline. It wasn't this.

So, after a funeral that only her immediate family could attend because of the Covid restrictions, Steuart is on his own, while a cohort of carers takes it in turns to look after him.

He seems happy with the draft of the book, happiest when he spots that I've mistyped his name in one sentence. Riddled with a cruel illness, he can still prod a finger at a mistake and smile. But the bouts of confusion seem to be longer and deeper. He keeps coming back to talking about *Paul Bunyan*.

'Are we going to do the overture?' he asks.

I'm flummoxed.

'We're going to open up the cut in Slim's aria. But I'm not so sure about the Lullaby of Dream Shadows after all . . .' Holding the manuscript of the memoir he says, 'Is this for the booklet?'

I cannot figure out what is going on. And then the penny drops.

During the 1980s Steuart started recording Britten's works for Collins Classics and he was making significant progress through the catalogue when the record label went bust. For Steuart this wasn't a vanity project, but his opportunity to put onto disc Britten's music in performances the composer would have approved of. He was even asked to record *Death in Venice* again, digitally for the first time, with Philip Langridge as Aschenbach. But as he told me at the time, 'Why would I want to record it again? I've already recorded it once. I told them they should get somebody else to do it.'

I suspect that the conversations we have had about *Paul Bunyan* have sparked a longing to get down on disc a definitive version of the operetta, with cuts restored and the whole piece shaped in a way that Steuart is convinced that Britten would have liked. But it's too late, and it's frustrating to be left only to imagine what a good case for the piece Steuart would have made.

THIRTEEN

And now, Phaedrus, I will go

In the months before the 1975 Aldeburgh Festival, Steuart conducted Donizetti's Torquato Tasso in London, and A Midsummer Night's Dream in Copenhagen (in Danish, with a baritone singing Oberon). The Aldeburgh Festival saw a revival of Death in Venice and the premiere of the Suite on English Folk Tunes.

◊

WHILE WE WERE MEETING to prepare for the BBC recording of *Paul Bunyan* in the spring of 1975, Ben first showed me his new *Suite on English Folk Tunes*, which he wanted me to conduct at the next Aldeburgh Festival.

The opening number, 'Cakes and Ale', is extremely tricky, and at the first rehearsal Ben suddenly decided that he wanted a brief '*Luftpause*' after each of the first three string solos (violin, viola and cello), an idea that we all found very hard to assimilate and that has caused problems ever since. The first performance was at a special gala concert for Queen Elizabeth, The Queen Mother, on Friday, 13 June. A second performance followed on 19 June in an entirely different programme, when Theodor Uppman sang 'Billy in the Darbies' from *Billy Budd*, the role he had created at Covent Garden in 1951. At the end of this aria there was originally a bottom F for the two horns, which in the 1961 revision had been transferred to the double-bass. The horns were very anxious to play the bottom F, but Ben was quite firm, saying that though it might be feasible, he did not think it would produce the sort of sound that he wanted. Unfortunately, we could not put this to the test, as Ben was not able to come to a rehearsal to hear them try it.

The English Opera Group, having revived *Death in Venice* for the 1975 Aldeburgh Festival and subsequently again at Covent Garden, had only one further production to offer before re-emerging as the English Music Theatre. This was a revival of *Curlew River* at the end of August 1975, the last time Ben was to see a Church Parable and the last time Peter was to sing the Madwoman.

Things seemed to be coming to an end; but Ben had just completed a new work, the cantata *Phaedra*, written for Janet Baker, and wanted me to see the score. As I sat in the Red House sitting room studying the pages, carefully observed by Ben, it was apparent that, whatever his physical condition, there was no falling off in his compositional powers. I asked him if I could direct the performance from the harpsichord, which functions very much as in eighteenth-century recitative, and he thought this a good idea provided I could have a little time alone with the cellist.

On 31 March 1976 Janet Baker and I met at the Red House library for a working session on the new piece. Ben was in excellent form and totally precise as to what he wanted. At the words 'I turned aside for shelter' he asked for the phrase to cloud over immediately and for 'Oh, it's nothing not to love' to be thrown away with a laugh. Occasionally he would change the odd note in the vocal line to clarify the declamation. Otherwise, he didn't say very much. Janet asked for a different note at one point, as she found it rather taxing, and he said, 'Oh yes, well, we'll do this', and he was very willing to change it. But he didn't have a lot to say by that stage. Having worked all the way through once, we gave a complete performance, and Ben seemed very satisfied.

The first orchestral rehearsal took place the day before the concert. As the string parts are extremely difficult, Ben gave us a little time to look over the notes before he appeared. Once there, he was immediately concerned with practical details. The bell at the opening had been notated an octave too high (i.e. at sounding pitch), and the bell we had was thus far too small. He was also very particular about the sound of the 'Ruthe' on the timpani at Fig. 5, and at Fig. 8 he stressed that the cymbals should be clashed, not suspended. In the initial stages we had serious problems getting into Fig. 22, until José-Luis García, the leader, suggested that the difficulty would be removed if we jettisoned the tie that originally joined the minim to the following semiquavers. We tried it, and it worked so well that Ben was quite happy to remove the offending tie.

The full programme consisted of Mozart's Symphony No. 33, *Phaedra*, *Doria* by Arne Nordheim (another world premiere, a setting of an Ezra Pound poem for tenor and orchestra – sung by Peter), and Strauss's suite *Le bourgeois gentilhomme* – a taxing programme for the orchestra. To add to the tension, the concert was broadcast by the BBC with a two-hour deferred relay, which meant we could tune in on the car radio on the way home.

The performance of *Phaedra* was a triumph for Ben and for Janet Baker, who was in top form – a real occasion. None of us realised that this would be the last time Ben would hear a premiere of his own work. He had barely six months left in which to complete the *Welcome Ode*. That and the Third String Quartet were both performed posthumously.

I was to see Ben once more only. On Friday, 1 October, the EMT brought its production of Mozart's *La finta giardiniera* to the Maltings. The following morning we had a meeting at the Red House to decide which opera we should do at the 1977 Festival. There was a potentially awkward situation in that the company wanted to do Purcell's *The Fairy Queen*, but not in the version that Ben had prepared for concert back in 1967, as this would have been very restricting for a full stage production. We could not be sure that Ben and Peter would see it that way, yet in the end there was no problem at all: they could not have been more understanding, and we parted full of hopes for the future.

◊

During November, Steuart was at Covent Garden, conducting *Così fan tutte* with a cast that included Kiri Te Kanawa, Thomas Allen and Norma Burrowes. Steuart's mother wrote to Britten and Pears on Britten's birthday, and Pears wrote back the next day:

> Ben is at ease, calm, clear, infinitely considerate and loving, a little weaker each day, in considerable discomfort but no great pain. We had a little champagne party on his birthday yesterday downstairs, & he sipping away upstairs – and each friend went up to say Goodbye. A lovely idea & worked so well. Now we wait but thankfully.
>
> [. . .]
>
> He will go on for ever in me.

I heard about Ben's death on the news. I knew things were not going well, that it wasn't long to go because I talked to Peter regularly, and we had fears about Ben's health for a long time. It did seem as if it was going to be the end.

Britten died in the early hours of 4 December 1976.

Steuart wrote to Pears, and at the end of his letter he said:

> Tonight's performance of *Paul Bunyan* will be dedicated to his memory; not, on the face of it, the most obvious choice of work but one which I personally believe would particularly rejoice his heart.
>
> We may indeed mourn his loss but how very much more will we treasure his memory.

Lesley, Steuart's mother, also wrote to Pears:

I wanted so much to tell you that for the 30 years that I knew Ben – though for many of those years I saw him seldom – he has been the major source of everything beautiful in my life. Even to have known and loved him and been in the influence of that dear personality would have been more than enough, but Steuart is the most precious thing in the world to me and what Ben gave to him is utterly beyond words to tell. I know that conducting those glorious works has made him the person he is, and I believe all his life the important thing will be to go on giving them to the world as he knows Ben would wish to hear them.

Two weeks later Steuart found himself on television, as a guest on the musical quiz show *Face the Music*, where the host Joseph Cooper tried to catch him out by playing a passage from *Death in Venice* on his trademark dummy keyboard.

◊

AFTER BEN DIED we were all bereft, not quite sure how we were going to carry on with the Aldeburgh Festival. Of course Peter took over the management, really, and he brought in Murray Perahia too.

The crucial thing for me was what we were going to do with the English Opera Group. By 1976 it had changed itself into the English Music Theatre. The problem had been that without Ben supplying new works for the group to perform it was in danger of losing its raison d'être, so we felt somehow we had to rejuvenate it or reactivate it, and if necessary rename the company. The idea was to recreate it as a touring organisation, which would consist of something like fifteen orchestral players and fifteen singers performing mostly new work around the provinces as well as in London. That was the scheme, and the Arts Council of Great Britain in their wisdom voted for this scheme. But then the Touring Arts Council Committee wouldn't accept it unless we also performed some standard opera. Of course this meant a much bigger orchestra and a much bigger group of singers. If you're going to do *The Magic Flute*, it's a different story. That split within the Arts Council was never actually resolved, and it eventually ended up with the disbandment of the company completely. They decided to pull the plug, but we did have two very eventful seasons. Having done *Paul Bunyan* in 1976 and 1977, we reappeared in Aldeburgh with *The Fairy Queen* with a very good production indeed, with dialogue and virtually all of Purcell's music.

I remember going down for a Festival Committee meeting where Peter had drawn up a sort of draft schedule and there wasn't a note of Ben's at all. We got some in, of course, and I did point this out. 'We must have some Ben, come on! We can't leave him out altogether.'

This was one of the strange things about Peter; again the enigmatic personality, you never quite knew. Most people found it very strange that when Ben was really ill, at the last minute, Peter didn't come buzzing back from Canada immediately. He just kept on doing his concerts, which was quite a surprise given he and Ben were lifetime partners.

Peter could be quite difficult. Dealing with him over the Festival was sometimes quite a prickly experience. If you suddenly wanted to do something in particular he might say, 'Oh no, for God's sake no.' He'd suddenly take a down against something and he wouldn't have anything to do with it. And there was all this business when the Britten–Pears School did Tchaikovsky's *Eugene Onegin* with Mstislav Rostropovich conducting in 1979. Peter had proclaimed that there would be no more opera at Aldeburgh, but *Onegin* had already been planned by the School – a great production as it turned out – which Peter suddenly decided he didn't want. Eventually, somebody had the brainwave of inviting him to do Monsieur Triquet, and all difficulties disappeared suddenly, overnight. It was also probably the only time Triquet has ever taken the final curtain call in *Onegin*.

Ben was the most important single musical influence in my life. I can speak of him only as I found him – a stern critic, both with himself and others, but always fair, clear thinking, and immensely practical, one who would never spare himself or compromise his own ideals and who with all his prodigious gifts had a touching humility.

Of course, I didn't realise, being younger, that I was taking part in something of historical importance. I should have kept diaries but I didn't.

Perhaps one day I too would have outlived my usefulness, but he was a creative artist needing to move on. He drained one source dry and moved on. He realised he was doing it but – for his development – he had to do that. Terrible scars were born by people who were hurt by this. For singers it was very hard. He hated doing it.

For myself, I found Ben easy to work with. I suspect it was because if he suggested anything I took a lot of trouble to do it. He very often found himself suggesting something to someone and they might have thought they were doing it but it didn't make any difference. And this always used to rile him.

However, for me, working with this great, great man was nothing but a privilege. And I liked him. I always did, right from the beginning. I was immediately attracted to that personality. I was always able to see his playful side, even later. It was there still, deep down. It was difficult to tap it but every so often it did come out.

I was once asked if I thought Ben was happy. I think he was too conscious of his artistic responsibility to enjoy happiness in the conventional sense. I'm not sure that you could exactly say that he was a happy man. He was doing what he was put on this earth to do and if he had his own doubts about it, there's no question that what he was doing was very wonderful.

He was brought up in a rather puritanical way. His mother was a very, very strong influence on him and she had him toe the line, no doubt taught him the virtue of humility, and she would have left him with a legacy of being very hard on himself, very self-critical. And I'm sure boys of his generation were taught never to show off. Going onto a platform to conduct is a form of showing off, and that upbringing was very much at odds with his practical life, the life he chose and needed to live by his very nature.

It's interesting that there were some pieces he didn't particularly want to own. The *American Overture* [1941], for instance; he never believed he'd written it. And if he did, he didn't want to know about it. It might have coincided with an unhappy time of his life, or a bad period, of which there were many.

Gloriana – which with *Grimes* was the only opera I never went through with him – was the worst time, when everyone seemed to have it in for him. The jealousy among the profession as well. The feeling that perhaps Lord Harewood had steered the commission his way, and then, when it didn't turn out as perhaps they thought it ought to turn out . . . Firstly, the audience was simply not expecting a serious work; they were expecting something like *Merrie England* – Edward German, that sort of thing – but they got a really serious piece and they didn't know what to make of it. And of course everybody was wearing gloves because it was a big royal occasion, so no applause could be heard. It was the most disastrous occasion, the wrong occasion to do that piece. To have survived that is quite something, though his hatred of critics never left him!

Ben never gave me technical advice on conducting. He certainly never had any conducting lessons. I mean what's a conducting lesson supposed to do? How do you teach anybody? But if someone asks me to go through a Britten piece, I always try to do it. When you go through, say, the operas, you see how beautifully they are put together. I always try to keep to exactly what the score is telling you, which is one hell of a lot. If you open any of Ben's scores and look at the vocal line for just four bars, you'll find there's all sorts of things there – legatos, accents – the relation from one bar to the next. But first and foremost, he did like people to get the notes right.

'*Grimes* on the Beach', 2013.

'Finally, we get to put the conductor where he belongs, in a hole in the ground.'

Top Celia and Steuart, Florence, 1978.
Below Celia with Jo and Charmian, 1987.

Celia and Steuart, Aldeburgh beach, 2016.

Steuart Bedford with his conducting score of *Death in Venice*,
at his home in Yoxford, 2018.

Steuart with one of his grandsons, Alun, by the Moot Hall, Aldeburgh, 2020.

Ben was eating an ice very slowly and with the intense concentration of a small boy.

'Just look at Ben's technique with an ice!' said Joan Cross.

'He looks like all my small boys rolled into one,' [Lesley] said. 'That's why I love him.'

Aldeburgh, June 2013

For many people, the outstanding event of Britten's centenary celebrations was 'Grimes on the Beach' – three performances during the
Aldeburgh Festival of *Peter Grimes,* performed 'on location', directed
by Tim Albery, designed by Leslie Travers, and conducted by Steuart.
A long stage of scaffolding, duckboards and old fishing boats was built on
the shingle, with the North Sea churning behind and George Crabbe's actual
so-called Borough, Aldeburgh itself, to the land side of the beach. Audiences
were thrilled not only by the music and the spectacle, but by being placed
right among the natural elements that are crucial to the opera: the sea, the
sky and the shingle beneath them, where they sat, wrapped against the chill
of the evening sea breeze.

    Musically, there were many challenges. Chief among these was the impos-
sibility of having a live orchestra. An orchestral track had to be recorded in
advance, but this created a new set of problems.

    At many places in the score there are pauses or *colla voce* markings,
where the conductor follows the singer rather than vice versa. How could
that possibly work if the orchestral track was set in stone? Steuart went
through the score with the recording producer, identifying stop–start points,
where, in an orchestral silence, a new 'track' could begin on his downbeat.

    Given that all the tempi for the opera would have to be set in advance,
how would the singers keep in time with the orchestral track? Steuart
reconducted the piece in time to the orchestra, cueing and managing the
singers.

    But how would he know what the exact tempo was? While Steuart re-
corded the entire opera with just the orchestra, he was simultaneously
filmed on video. Then, at the performances, he watched himself on the video
feedback and relayed the beat back to the singers and made sure everyone on stage was singing not only together, but with the orchestral track.
It meant that there was no room for error. If someone went astray, there

was nothing Steuart could do with the orchestra – increase or decrease the tempo, for instance – to get everyone back into the same place.

To manage all this, and to place Steuart in the traditional spot where the singers would be used to watching the conductor, they had to dig an actual pit, about three feet down into the shingle, in which they buried a hutch, big enough to take three or four men, standing, and a large amount of technical equipment. The hutch was then given a corrugated iron roof. From the audience it looked like a winch cover, or a place to store fishing nets. (It also allowed me a joke at Steuart's expense: 'Finally, we get to put the conductor where he belongs, in a hole in the ground.')

Inside the hutch was Steuart – he had to climb down a short ladder. He could be seen from the waist up, sometimes battling to stop his score blowing away in the wind, in front of him a television monitor cased in a wooden box. With him were a producer, a sound engineer and, sometimes, an assistant. This was where they stayed for the entirety of the opera.

The second performance was the only night when the weather was threatening. There was a low bank of cloud, and an occasional bout of fine drizzle that could be mistaken for sea spray in the theatre spotlights. It was cold.

I was singing the part of Horace Adams, the Rector. At the start of Act III I would wait backstage, just a few feet from the sea's edge, before climbing a steep flight of steps and launching into my little song about roses. Because it was cold that night, I took refuge in a small garden shed that had been erected as a shelter from inclement weather. Inside was a TV monitor, its feed a camera pointed at Steuart in the pit.

Act III opens with the sublime 'Moonlight' Sea Interlude, which manages not only to capture the slowly rocking swell of the North Sea but the flecks of moonlight bouncing off its surface. I could imagine the view from the audience and how magical it must be – the stage, the boats, the music, the sea itself quietly joining in with whispers of waves on shingle.

I looked up at the TV monitor. There was Steuart, not conducting. He didn't have to – the recording was playing, there was nobody on stage to cue.

He was dressed, not in white tie and tails as an opera audience might expect, but in a warm fleece and a large, padded anorak. His thinning white hair was tousled by the wind, his head swaying slowly to the music. He turned a page of his score, and then nonchalantly reached into a Tupperware container next to the sound engineer, picked out a biscuit and took a bite, the horns of the orchestra swelling as he chewed on his chocolate hobnob.

It was quite wonderful.

No epilogue, I pray you, for your play needs no excuse

(A Midsummer Night's Dream)

This book was supposed to end with '*Grimes* on the Beach'.

In August of 2020 Steuart read the second draft and prodded triumphantly at the typos he had found, but in the months that followed, his health deteriorated so much that he was barely able to contribute. I continued to work on the book, and on 12 February 2021, I sent in my final notes from the publisher's proof, hoping desperately that the book would be printed in time for Steuart to hold a copy.

Three days later, Charmian Bedford rang to tell me her dad had died, peacefully, that morning.

It's a curious task, to co-author a memoir. There have been times when I've envied biographers who have the luxury of a deceased subject, for they can speculate freely on their subject's journey – what caused this, what motivated them to do that.

With Steuart this was out of the question. If ever I tried, he rewarded me with an 'I'm not so sure about that.' Latterly, when he struggled to find words, this became a sort of pop-popping sound he made with his lips, his brow furiously furrowed, but I knew what it meant.

There are only a couple of places in the book that I have put words into Steuart's mouth, crafted from the many discussions we had. He queried me on one in particular.

'Did I say that?'

'Well, not exactly, but I asked you about it and this paraphrases what we discussed. Do you want me to take it out?'

'No, actually I rather like it.'

I'm going to miss Steuart so much – his bony hug, his beloved insults. During one of my visits I was searching for the right bin in the kitchen to recycle a cardboard box.

'Steuart, where can I stick this?'

'Up your arse.'

Charming.

I'm going to miss his curmudgeonly geniality, his absolute kindness, that he trusted me to do this, that he blessed me with this curious task. And of course I'm going to miss Steuart the musician, one of our very last direct connections with Britten, and a conductor cut from a cloth they really don't make any more.

Although he hasn't been physically able to collaborate in the last few months, in my head I've still needed Steuart's permission for every decision I've made. As the ever diligent conductor who has prepared his cast meticulously, I can hear him telling me, 'Shape it. Don't be extravagant. Don't get flouncy. And for God's sake, get the bloody notes right.'

Acknowledgements

Our foremost debt of thanks is to Britten Pears Arts, owner of the copyright in much of the material in this book, in particular countless letters and photographs. In particular we would like to thank Sarah Bardwell, the Executive Director, for her hugely generous support of this project, and Dr Christopher Hilton (Head of Archive and Library) and Dr Nicholas Clark (Librarian) for their extraordinary work and help. The Britten–Pears Archive at the Red House is an outstanding and beautiful library, full of extraordinary resources, and staffed by people of dedication and deep knowledge. Despite the Covid-19 pandemic and the library's closure to regular visits, the librarians went to great lengths to keep the archive accessible; without them, the tireless Nicholas Clark in particular, the completion of this book would have been impossible.

The authors would also like to thank Philip Reed and Jill Burrows of the Bittern Press for their expert help, guidance and encouragement.

We would also like to thank James Bowman, David Kimbell and Sebastian Kraemer for their contributions, Lady Mary Ledger for permission to share a passage from Sir Philip Ledger's memoir, and Norma Burrowes for her support, recollections and photographs.

Our personal thanks go to Lucy Schaufer, John Perry, Charmian Bedford, Jo Bedford, and the entire Bedford family; also to Lucy Walker and Oliver Soden for insights and encouragement; and of course and especially to Celia Bedford, to whom this book is dedicated.

S.B. C.G.

Index

186